A Clean, Well-Lighted Stream

A Clean, Well-Lighted Stream

Michael Checchio

Contents

Chapters were previously published in somewhat different form in
the following periodicals: California Fly Fisher, Fly Rod & Reel,
The Flyfisher, San Francisco Focus, Gray's Sporting Journal.

Copyright © 1992, 1993, 1994, 1995 by Michael Checchio
All rights reserved under International and Pan-American
Copyright Conventions. Printed in China. Published in the
United States of America by

Soho Press, Inc.
853 Broadway
New York, N.Y. 10003

Book design by Cheryl L. Cipriani

Library of Congress Cataloging-in-Publication Data
Checchio, Michael, 1951–
  A clean, well-lighted stream / Michael Checchio.
     p. cm.
  ISBN 1-56947-045-6 (alk. paper)
   1. Trout fishing—California—Anecdotes.   2. Trout fishing—
Northwest, Pacific—Anecdotes.   3. Checchio, Michael, 1951–
I. Title.
SH688.U6C48   1995
818'.5403—dc20
  [B]   *95-30347*
                                          CIP

A Clean, Well-Lighted Stream

Tracks
in the Water

Dawn. The redwoods are cold, vaporous and dripping. We are on the banks of an isolated Northern California steelhead stream shortly after one of the first rains of winter and the black-green pools mirror the great canopy of the forest, almost imploring you to wade in and fish. In the half-light, the canyon resembles a Japanese woodcut of bank willows and river mist. The fishing is a little Zen-like, too: more fishing than fish, it would seem.

I make another sweeping cast of the pool. The cold green water presses against my waders, the river surging inexorably toward the ocean less than two miles away. Beside me is yet another fly fisherman making similarly long, searching casts with considerably more finesse. His line unrolls in tight loops along a perfect plane, behind and then in front, and then shoots crisply to the other side of the river, as if reaching for a larger world.

Downstream in a pool below a flue of rushing water, a rod bends deeply and an angler is fast to a steelhead, the great trout of the Pacific Ocean. This is the first fish anyone has struck all morning. I watch the fortunate angler as he plays the huge fish that saws back and forth in the river. Finally the steelhead is beached, a prize of, say, eleven pounds, so fresh and bright it seems like a shining hubcap washed up on the gravel bank.

The remainder of the morning passes without another strike. By now the mist has burned off and the sun penetrates the redwoods in shafts of cathedral light. Someone has built a fire and I walk over to warm my hands. By now everyone is standing around complaining about the drought, the dams, the strip-logged hills and the truly spectacular absence of fish. Clearly, somewhere along the line, we Californians have been locked out of Paradise. Whining helps when confronted with a remote and unproductive Lost Coast stream in the northern tier of the state.

If you are new to the San Francisco Bay area, as I am, and learning to fly-fish for winter steelhead, then sooner or later you find yourself on the banks of the Russian River in Sonoma County. You are not here because the fishing is any good but because the Russian is the nearest major steelhead river north of the city. It is a day trip.

The Russian is a paradox: the best of streams and the worst. I first saw it on a November afternoon through sun-shot mist, wilting grapevines and dark redwood groves. Its banks were overdeveloped, its riverbed festooned with litter. I spent the first day trying to gain access through private property adjacent to streets with names like Steelhead Lane and Freezeout.

On a subsequent warm December day I went out to fish the great sweeping bend at Villa Grande. My line shot out over the pool, but the fly died the moment it hit the water. Where the hell was the current? It was the drought, of course. The sandbar at the mouth was blocked, the river actually backing up. Normally the rains that begin in December have flushed the riverbed and blown out the bar by now. Regrettably, California was entering yet another straight year of drought.

Over a hundred sea lions formed a line at the mouth at Jenner, waiting for steelhead to run the gauntlet when the river rose.

Another morning found me upriver at Bud Hole, watching nine anglers casting shoulder to shoulder to a single indifferent steelhead resting deep beneath the willow sweepers on the far bank. To get away from the crowd, I bushwhacked downstream one mile, searching for some decent holes. What I found instead was an enormous grade of flattened sand and gravel, the size of six football fields. It had once held trees and streamside vegetation. You could still see the marks of the dozer blade in the furrowed ground.

Later, at my friend Hal's place we talked about what had befallen the river.

"The Russian was one of the greatest steelhead rivers in the world," Hal assured me. "It had runs of over a hundred thousand fish at one time, and that wasn't so long ago, either."

"That's hard to picture," I said. We were in his North Beach apartment sipping beers and watching the sun disappear beyond the Golden Gate.

Hal is a fly fisherman and, that rarity, a native Californian. He is a man who takes the despoiling of his state's watershed personally. Hal holds to a very narrow view of the twentieth century and while he likes to complain about things such as "Yosemite National Parking Lot" and refers to the U.S. Forest Service as "that wholly owned subsidiary of the lumber industry," he has never once joined an environmental organization or even purchased a California fishing license. Naturally his chief scorn is reserved for his fellow anglers, of whom he believes there are far too many. I like to think of him as the Antichrist of fly fishing. The day he first told me about the ravaging of the Russian, he became so angry I thought he would blow a blood vessel. In a voice raw with outrage, Hal explained how the once magnificent fishery had suffered a near-total collapse.

Vineyards had sprung up along the spawning tributaries, diverting the waters for irrigation and the nurturing of grapes for blush wine manufacture. Then came developers and the disgorgement of raw sewage right into the river. And long before that there had been construction of dams and short-sighted timbering practices in the headwaters. Clear-cutting erodes hillsides; silt pours into rivers when it rains, covering gravel beds upon which steelhead and salmon spawn. Dams, in addition to impeding fish migration, slow a river's natural flow and impair the ability of the river to scour the bottom clean. The run of wild silver salmon on the Russian is almost extinct. The steelhead run, too, is down to mostly artificially bred hatchery fish. Very few wild steelhead reproduce in the Russian.

Still, a seventeen-pounder was hoisted out of the river below Monte Rio one recent January. And there are a few places free of the scourge of bankside development. All's not lost, as they say. On midwinter evenings, as the light drains off the riverbanks, a few steelhead stir in the gloom. On nights like these, it's almost possible to forget that in the onetime redneck river town of Guerneville there now seem to be as many gay bars as there are in San Francisco. Or that nearby is the Bohemian Grove, a private redwood reserve where every summer the richest and most powerful white males in America—

ex-presidents, cabinet members and captains of finance—convene to get drunk outdoors and run naked as newts, peeing on the trees and lady ferns. Remember, all this takes place in California.

So you are standing in the middle of a river risking hypothermia, your expensive neoprene waders leaking, and all for what? A creature that can't even call itself a mammal. A cold-blooded salmonid.

Steelhead are sea-run rainbow trout. Like salmon, steelhead are anadromous, from the Greek for "running upward." Born in fresh river water, steelhead migrate to the vast dining halls of the Pacific between their first and third years. There they roam between the continents; fish tagged on the West Coast have been caught off the waters of Russia's Kamchatka Peninsula. Steelhead are aptly named too: their upper bodies turn steel blue while at sea, their sides bright silver. And their common name implies an inner toughness, like a Pittsburgh Steelers running back or steel mill worker in western Pennsylvania.

At the onset of sexual maturity, after one to three years of feasting in the open waters, steelhead return to spawn in the very river—some believe the very pool—where they were born. They recognize their natal stream by the river's indelible trace elements and singular chemical composition and pursue its scent like bloodhounds following footprints through water.

Steelhead are at their prime once they enter fresh water. But soon the river begins to wash out their sea metal colors. As steelhead prepare to spawn, their backs turn from metallic blue to mottled olive and on their silvery sides appears the rosy band of a rainbow trout.

Steelhead inhabit West Coast streams roughly from Monterey north to Alaska. They will idle in the rivers for months before ascending the tributary creeks to begin the actual spawning rites.

It is considered bad manners to fish over a mating couple during courtship (and is even illegal on many of California's tributaries). In an upper pool, a male and female pair off. Using her body and tail to brush away river gravel, the female digs a redd, or nest, and deposits her eggs. The male then darts in and fertilizes the eggs with his cloudy milt. This underwater pas de deux is repeated over several redds until the hen fish has surrendered all her eggs. Unlike all Pacific salmon—which die after their first spawning run, literally starving themselves to death in their mission to reproduce, digesting all stored-up fat and muscle tissue, even the final protein in their fins and scales—many steelhead survive to make the journey from ocean to river and back again several times. Such a steelhead returning to the sea is called a kelt. Spent and starving, the descending kelts can appear as thin as pikestaffs, and again, it is bad form to fish for them when they are in this exhausted stage of their migratory loop.

Fresh from the ocean, they are fair game. Surging upriver on enormous reserves of stored energy, the steelhead will pause to rest in the cover of the deeper riffles or the tailouts of pools. Whereas salmon tend to mill about the bottom of the deeper pools, circling restlessly in aqueous daisy chains, steelhead face upstream, holding themselves in the current with epic poise. It is here they can be induced into taking a carefully swung fly, lure or "berry" of roe. When intercepted, steelhead fight with more strength, panic and high-jumping abandon than any salmonid in any Pacific Northwest river, including king salmon, which can be twice their size. With the sexual imperative upon them, never has life held such urgency. To connect with a steelhead at this moment, to feel its cosmic surge jump through the rod into your body, is like taking the pulse of the planet.

Classic pools and dramatic winter fish. The music of the spheres. What else could one ask for? Well, in California, you might ask for fewer people.

About a year ago, my friend Hal suggested we hang it up on the Russian and try a "real" steelhead river instead. He proposed a short and pretty coastal river called the Gualala (pronounced Waa la la) that winds like a green streamer through an icy redwood canyon on the border of Sonoma and Mendocino counties. Hal assured me that, although it was only one hundred fourteen miles from San Francisco, it was so isolated and the ride up the Pacific Coast Highway so tortuous that we could be assured of getting a pool to ourselves on a weekday.

When we got there, it seemed as if every fly fisherman with a license had already shouldered his way into the tailout of Miner Hole. It was the same up and down the river. The pools were as crowded as the freeways at rush hour.

"I don't believe this," muttered my friend, who was not prepared to resign himself to the situation with egalitarian elan.

At Sonoma County Park on the south shoreline, where trails in the redwood grove lead upstream to many of the famous pools, there was barely any room left among the parked cars, vans and four-wheel drives. Upstream at Thompson Hole, the hardware fishermen (who had hacked down bank alders and willows with machetes) were drifting baits and slowly retrieving spoons through the deepest lies. At the Donkey Hole, the fly fishermen crowding the gravel bar crossed lines with the rock plunkers on the far shore. The river seemed equally divided between the spinning and bait-casting crowd perched on the cliffs and the fly-fishing mob, waist-deep and double-hauling in the green flow. The lines of the latter passed back and forth through the air in long elegant loops with swing and distinct visual appeal. I remarked as much to my friend. He stared back at me with eyes like rat poison pellets.

To him the bait fishermen perching on the rocks are jackanapes. They kill all the fish they catch and leave their borax-dusted bait, their maline mesh and monofilament tangles behind on the banks in stinking piles. The fly fishermen are worse. They believe their style of fishing confers privilege. Their equipment is exorbitantly expensive and they covet famous rivers as if they were designer logos. Hal began fly fishing decades ago, when it was a true crank's passion, not the pastime of overachieving yuppies, so I was not inclined to share my companion's uncharitable view of our brotherhood of the angle. I badly wanted to catch a steelhead. I asked Hal what he thought our chances were in this bouillabaisse of flashy humanity.

"Exactly what you'd think," he snapped.

We waded into Miner Hole, the other fishermen nodding warily to us. Clearly no one would be observing any of the polite ceremonies of Pacific Northwest fly fishing this day. On many legendary steelhead streams—say, the North Umpqua in Oregon or the Skykomish in Washington—fly-fishing etiquette has evolved over the years. Anglers are expected to fish through a pool once and then surrender it to give the next angler a chance at good water. The accepted protocol is to make a cast, take one step downstream and repeat, until the length of the pool has been traversed. In turn, according to this unwritten code, no one wades into the water directly below the working fisherman, spoiling his sport. The system works. Everyone gets to fish out an entire pool.

But here everyone bulls his way into the best places and casts into the same spot. Your bladder, not your conscience, tells you when it's time to get off the water.

So I joined the lineup and picked up the drill. Once in place, waist-deep alongside fifteen other anglers, I stripped line off my reel, cocked my wrist and drove what I thought was a massive cast straight across the green pool (but which characteristically fell short of everyone else's). The line sank and swung the fly in a slow-motion arc through the current. When the fly stopped downstream, straight below me, I made a few short, stripping retrieves to impart a little more action to it, as I had been instructed, then picked up and cast again. And again . . . for the next two hours.

There is a kind of monotonous sublimity to this work, I kept telling myself. My companion offered encouragement. "Where the hell did you learn how to cast?" he demanded.

By evening, I had falsely convinced myself I was going to catch a steelhead. Dusk seems to change everything on a river and I could feel an aura of radiation and silent promise. Gradually the canyon filled with a deep liquid darkness and energy. Directly below me, a steelhead rolled. And another one out beyond that. But it was an angler working well above Race Track Riffle who took the only fish that evening.

I stood with the others in the peanut gallery and watched the magnificent fish eased onto the beach to be admired and released. It looked like it could go twelve pounds, average for the river. It shone like a bar of silver. "Nice fish," said my friend, his eyes dangerous circles. The fishing was over for the night.

It is axiomatic that beside every fine trout stream there is a good saloon. So we went into the little town of Gualala for a drink. Our destination was the Gualala Hotel, a raffish fishing landmark as emblematic of the river as the steelhead themselves. Its bar was filled with locals, steelhead anglers and the pleasant din of conversation. The fate of the river seemed to be a frequent topic at the tables. A fellow angler engaged Hal in a spirited debate, defending hatchery fish. The angler invoked statistics and logic. As usual, Hal chose the ad hominem attack. I decided to take a stroll around the bar to look at the old Polaroids of sport catches taken over the years.

The town of Gualala, with its handful of service stations, real estate offices and new motels, is said to be losing its sense of coastal isolation with each passing season. The newspapers that winter were full of stories about Gualala, about its funny-sounding name, its remote beauty and the celebrities such as Robin Williams who were rumored to be buying property nearby. Steelhead, it seemed, weren't the only show species following a migratory pattern.

Next morning I was up early, examining white PVC tubes anchored to stakes in the river shallows. Here, I was told, lies the future of the Gualala. These tubes are fish traps designed to hold live captured steelhead for a volunteer hatchery project. The state supplements its wild steelhead runs by means of artificial culturing. ("When I hear the word 'aquaculture,' I reach for my revolver," says Hal, doing his best Hermann Göring impression.)

Hal is not alone in his contempt for hatchery fish. Fish and game officials love hatcheries because they give the public the illusion of cheap production and cost efficiency. But what my friend sees here is the shotgun wedding of biology and politics. The general public is duped into believing that tame hatchery fish can replace wild trout and somehow compensate for clear-cutting our forests, damming our rivers and destroying our watersheds.

Fish culture—underwater poultry farming, if you will—has vast appeal for state fishery managers and politicians. It purportedly produces the most trout in the shortest time at the lowest cost. For example, hatchery strains display surprisingly rapid growth. A wild, stream-bred steelhead, smolt normally, spends two years in fresh water. But hatchery technicians, selecting ripening eggs for early maturity, can send the fish packing off to sea in one year, thereby slashing costs. What comes back, sportsmen argue, is less than a true fish.

Trout-hatchery smolts raised in concrete rearing tanks and living on handouts of Purina Trout Chow (yes, it's really called that) simply are not adapted to recognize natural foods and predators once they are dumped into a river after a year's growth.

More alarmingly, some hatchery strains become hybrids, displaying characteristics of artificiality and mixed origin as queer as anything found in science fiction. Ripe females can carry fewer eggs and a disturbing number of their ova can be infertile. One generation of stunted fish breeds another. Such hybrids are no more like a stream trout or a wild steelhead than a chicken is like an eagle.

Moreover, each wild steelhead is genetically adapted to its own native stream. This means that a fish swimming in the waters of California's Eel River comes from a different race than those in the nearby Klamath, or Oregon's Rogue River, or the Babine in British Columbia. Each branch or tributary creek on a river may even produce its own unique strain of fish, too.

Only a small number of hatchery fish survive to spawn. Even fewer survive to spawn with wild fish. Yet the few that do can spread the genetic pollution to the wild stock, diluting the gene pool and weakening the overall population. Fish are replaceable; gene pools aren't.

Not everyone views it this darkly. The redoubtable Dick May, former head of the activist organization California Trout, doesn't see hatchery steelhead subduing the region's wild stocks. Brood stocks for hatchery steelhead come from fish that have already returned from the sea, May explains. These are fish that have already proven they have "some of the right stuff." When steelhead hatcheries are run not for mass production, as so many "trout plants" are, but with the limited goal of maintaining the viability of a particular steelhead run, there is less chance for genetic monkeying, less likelihood of producing, in May's words, "a pack of poodles instead of wolves." May points out that attrition among hatchery steelhead is so high that the majority don't even survive. Only a few dynamic and genetically sound hatchery steelhead make it back from the rigors of the ocean. May believes such steel head can be used as a temporary solution to restoring stream habitats and can even complement a wild run after rehabilitation is achieved.

Fortunately the hatchery project on the Gualala uses only brood stock from the river, thus preserving the pure Gualala River strain. This short river, which drops from the gentle Coastal Ranges and has about eleven miles of legal fishing water, boasts a run of between four and six thousand fish. Most are healthy, aggressive, some going up to eighteen pounds. The year I first fished the river, seven hens and nine bucks—the majority, wild fish—were taken from the traps for the hatchery project at Doty Creek on the river's north fork. The brood fish were milked of their milt and roe and then returned to the Gualala, presumably to cycle back through the river and migrate out to sea again. The fingerlings that hatched—about twenty-two thousand steelhead fry—were held in the hatchery ponds for a year to grow and then were released into the lower river as smolts the following March. At this point, they averaged less than a half-pound each. Their migration began almost immediately. Those that survived the sea lions and Asian drift nets were expected to return from the sea in three years.

Arch Richardson, who runs a country general store in nearby Stewarts Point, and who has fished the Gualala throughout four decades, has seen a tragic decline in wild steelhead on his river. Richardson, past president of the Gualala River Steelhead Project, the volunteer group that maintains the hatchery program under the oversight of California's Department of Fish and Game, estimates that ninety percent of the run on the lower river is now composed entirely of hatchery fish.

The hatchery project has saved the Gualala River steelhead from extinction, he says, but the goal is to phase out the hatchery. Richardson says the group's great challenge will be to restore natural stream habitat along the entire river and tributary system, returning the Gualala to its glory of forty years ago with runs composed exclusively of wild, stream-bred fish. This means improving gravel beds, providing adequate stream cover and, where necessary, narrowing upper-river channels to speed stream flow.

Wild steelhead need wild water: swift, cold and clean. What they get is often degraded, despoiled. A map of California's major river systems today is a catalog of environmental insult.

The great river systems begin for the most part in the Cascades and High Sierra as clear founts and cold rivulets, lacy falls and featherlike streams. Too often, they end in the surgical stumps of tail-races, pipelines, afterbays, forebays, canals, aqueducts and dead-water sloughs, each designed to quench the state's terrible thirst for agribusiness, flush its perpetually gurgling toilets and water its desert lawns. Beneath motionless blue reservoirs lie the drowned valleys of California.

"Will you look at that?" My friend Hal pointed his rod directly across the pool where we were fishing. A bank angler had landed a steelhead and was now dispatching his fish with a smart whack to the head.

I asked Hal, "You don't kill any of the steelhead you catch?"

"I'm a humanist. I'd sooner kill a man than a fish."

He was kidding, of course. I had eaten trout at his house more than once. I wasn't sure, though, if he had ever killed a man. There were days on the river when he seemed angry enough.

It was evening before my companion struck his first fish of our trip. Hal's rod dipped with sudden violence and bent in a tremendous bow. The reel screamed twice, and then, just as quickly as the fish had come on, the line went suddenly slack.

"It's hooking him that counts," said my friend, philosopher and liar.

I too longed to feel my own line come up tight and race with life. John Muir once wrote something to the effect that when you pull on a single thing in nature, you find it connected to the rest of the world. I too wanted to feel that tug. But every day it gets harder to make that metaphorical approach to the universe. I think of all that steelhead mean and all that man has done to them.

Even so, the canyon through which the Gualala flowed that last evening seemed somehow untouched by the hand of man, a hall of wonders guarded by cliffs of redwood, pine and an embroidery of fern stitched into the rock face. At the river's mouth, cypress, darker than the pines, seemed to burn softly like candles in a temple.

You always anticipate a steelhead, but somehow never quite believe it when the strike finally happens. In the late evening, a fish took my fly with a tremendous grab. The canyon had become a cold tunnel. Dark. At first there was an alarming sensation of being played by both the fish and the river at once, of not being in control. In that initial burst of panic, I cared little whether the steelhead was wild-bred or not, only that it fought with all the strength and resolution of its great Pacific journey home. In the end, I tailed the fish in the shallows and watched the river pour over its sea metals, its flank as cold and bright as a winter star. I eased the fish back into the current and let the river reclaim him.

Mendocino

The best bars in the world, as everyone knows, are in San Francisco. Not all of them; only the top forty or fifty. In all, there are just over a thousand places in town to buy a drink. I haven't been in each of them, although for a year I had dedicated myself to the goal. That was when I first moved to San Francisco and started fishing for winter steelhead.

I found that being a winter steelhead fisherman meant that you spent a lot of time hanging around bars waiting for the drought to end, or when the rains finally came, waiting for the rivers to clear. I wasn't working much at the time.

My favorite daytime hangout was Vesuvio's, a bar in North Beach that had been a frequent haunt of Kerouac's and the Beats' back in the fifties. It was here that I discovered Sierra Nevada Pale Ale, which is brewed in Chico, and saw poker dice played for the first time. Now here was something an Easterner like me could get into—rolling for drinks with the bartender. To my ears, the slap of the leather cups and the clatter of dice across the mahogany called up the red light of the Barbary Coast, with its shanghaied sailors, whorehouses and waterfront deadfalls.

Occasionally, I would tire of the bohemian saloons of North Beach and walk up Grant Avenue into Chinatown, doing my best to act like a good tourist. There on Grant, I found a dark stone cave called Li Po, named after China's exquisite lyric poet, who is said to have drowned in a river while drunkenly contemplating the moon's reflection. I would pass under the huge painted lantern that hangs from the ceiling and sit directly across from the serene Buddha in its golden shrine behind the bar. There I would sip mixed drinks and talk to Alice, the beautiful Eurasian bartender.

Sometimes I would drift into the Tenderloin, the spiritual epicenter of the city. The Tenderloin is a dismal neighborhood of flophouses, porn theaters and soup lines, and boasts some of the grimiest but liveliest bars in the Western Hemisphere. I found it irresistible. These were the same streets Dashiell Hammett, my favorite San Francisco author, walked as a private detective, the same cheap boarding-house rooms where he wrote *The Maltese Falcon*. It was the kind of neighborhood where you could walk into a derelict bar like Jowell's on the corner of Ellis and Jones and find paperbacks by Ayn Rand and John Dos Passos resting on a windowsill. In Harrington's, a dimly lit dive on Larkin, I spent a pleasant afternoon drinking beers with Abie Chapman, the last living member of Murder Incorporated. Abie was a Chicago hood who wound up in Alcatraz and liked the view of San Francisco so much he stayed.

Later, when I got to know the town better, I found myself in some of its more obscure neighborhoods. The oddest was a place called Dogpatch, a run-down industrial tract near the China Basin shipyards. Here were real working-men's bars straight out of *On the Waterfront*, with names like Bouncer's, Tugboat Annie's, the Main Mast and my favorite—Tom's Dry Dock. It was in the Dry Dock that I met an out-of-work shipwright named Henry Corsmo and his defense attorney. The two were celebrating Corsmo's latest DUI conviction. They had been in the bar for some time, shooting pool for Budweisers (no doubt they would be sadder Budweiser men in the morning—an old joke) and for the lawyer's fee. Corsmo broke hard but didn't play for shape. And so the lawyer did what he was unable to do in court—he won—and pocketed his fee. It had just doubled. "Have a nice day," he said, reaching for his overcoat.

"Don't tell me what kind of day to have," Corsmo snapped.

The lawyer laughed. "You might have won if you hadn't told the jury you had a 'knack' for alcoholism and could drive while drunk." The guy put on his coat and headed for the door.

Corsmo looked over at me for a long moment and then said, "Game?"

"Okay."

He flipped me a quarter for the rack. We played for beers and were pretty much even after a half-dozen games. Afterward, we sat at a table and drank our prizes under the faded prints of old naval campaigns that decorated the dingy walls. We talked about everything and nothing: the depressed shipwright business, the San Francisco Forty-Niners, our favorite bars and the women who were walking into the Dry Dock with less regularity than we would have preferred. Quite by accident, I mentioned how much I wanted to get out of the city and do a little steelheading. Which it turned out was just about the one thing Henry Corsmo lived for.

"I got off jury duty once by claiming steelhead fishing as my religion," said Corsmo, "but weirdness only goes so far, even in San Francisco."

"More likely you were bumped because of your rap sheet."

We quarreled mildly over whether shooting heads or weight-forward tapers would best get the job done. I told him I was a steelhead tyro, that I had been fishing on the Russian River and doing dismally. That I had also been on the Gualala, but was put off by the crowds. It was then that Henry Corsmo offered to do something extremely out of character. He offered to take me to a favorite steelhead river, the Navarro, one of those dramatic redwood streams in Mendocino County that, despite its proximity to San Francisco, gets relatively light use. We made immediate plans to hit the river. I would pick Corsmo up at dawn three days hence. It was only after I left the Dry Dock that I realized the motive behind his offer to show a complete stranger his favorite steelhead holes. Corsmo had just had his driver's license rudely jerked from his grasp by a judge no doubt unduly concerned with public safety and I was to be his free ride.

Whatever our fortunes on the Navarro might prove to be, there would still be the pleasure of driving through the Anderson Valley to get there. I had been looking forward to it.

Henry was sober and clear-eyed, having assured me that fishing with a hangover was for amateurs. At Cloverdale we turned west on SR 128 and headed for Boonville, the tiny commercial center of the remote Anderson Valley, best known as the home of an obscure language called Boontling. It turned out that my passenger had grown up here, had cousins still living in Boonville and he knew the Navarro River as intimately as the burst capillaries in his face. Henry happily filled me in on the finer points of Boontling as we drove.

Boontling originated near the end of the nineteenth century as a game of verbal one-upmanship among local teenage boys trying to best each other through newly invented slang. Within a few years, the coining of new words became a seriocomic business. It was picked up by younger brothers and sisters, girlfriends and later wives and children, and gradually Boontling became the "native tongue" of the valley's five hundred residents. Among the chief pleasures of "harpin boont" was speaking to one another in the presence of outsiders without being understood by them.

The limited vocabulary of Boontling was taken from midland American dialects and community names, familiar sounds and the corruption of other tongues, mainly Spanish and the local Pomo Indian.

"Pie was called 'Charlie Brown,' after a farmer who ate it after every meal," explained Corsmo. "The phone is called a 'Walter' because the first person to have one installed here was Walter Levy."

Animals were renamed for the sounds they made. Thus squirrels became "squeakyteeks." "Gorm"—to eat—was taken from the French *gourmand*. And so on. Boontling is peppered with "nonch harpins"—objectionable talk. The word for fucking (not on the vocabulary list at Anderson Elementary) is "ricky chow."

"Don't even ask where that one comes from," said Corsmo.

Boontling died out during the First World War, when many residents moved out of the valley. The language was saved from oblivion, however, with the formation of the Boontlingers' Club in the early 1960s. The revival caught on and Boontling was actually taught to little kids in Anderson Valley Elementary School.

We stopped to drink coffee and gorm some breakfast as soon as we hit Boonville. There I bought a copy of the *Anderson Valley Advertiser*, one of American journalism's true curiosities. The *Anderson Valley Advertiser* is a country version of an underground urban newspaper, a combination of rural community journal and left-wing radical rag. My copy was studded with epigrams from Lenin, Thomas Babington Macaulay and Cato the Elder. It's important to remember that the Anderson Valley's principal exports are timber, apples and the world's best marijuana, not necessarily in that order.

The publisher was a fiercely quarrelsome newspaperman whose brand of journalism came straight out of the classic Western school of intense personal vituperation. He had little time for the boring yet reassuring trivia that is the staple of most small-town newspapers. He preferred to savage reactionaries on the school board or take apart some particularly otiose state legislator rather than cover the latest chicken pie fête being put on by the Grange. He had once printed on the front page, in the midst of the coverage of a murder trial, a cartoon diagraming the deputy district attorney's brain. A space was marked "hole in the ozone layer." I began to see why living and fishing in California was such a deeply eccentric enterprise.

More to the point, I knew the *Anderson Valley Advertiser* had been in the vanguard of reporting on the timber wars raging in the state's Redwood Empire. If the Navarro River was filled with silt today—as it frequently was—readers would know just who was to blame: Louisiana Pacific, which had carved a swath of destruction through Northern California by engaging in the most rapacious over-cutting in the annals of American forestry.

We rode on, past hills clustered with live oak and madrone, apple orchards and vineyards, until we came to the coastal redwood forest where the Navarro cut like a sword of light through the trees. At Corsmo's direction, I pulled into a turnout and we walked through the ferns and towering redwoods toward the riverbank. The Navarro was narrow and confined here, the steep banks tight with brush and willows. The river gurgled against the banks as if pouring through the neck of a bottle. The only way to fly-fish this stretch would be to roll cast, my least favorite method. From our high vantage we gazed down into the narrow band of water. Midmorning luminescence flooded the gorge. Corsmo pointed to a green chamber on the outside curve where three small steelhead held motionless, as if suspended.

"We'll swim the flies right down into the slots," said Corsmo.

We suited up, assembled our rods and bushwhacked upstream. The river was a bit high from a recent rain. I stepped into the cold water and instantly felt the current wrap around my legs.

"You go first," Corsmo said.

A fine-grained vapor flew off my line as I roll cast toward the far bank. The fly sank slowly and slid into the deep throat of the run.

"Mend your line," Corsmo said.

I did. The fly continued on its grave mission down the slot. Just as it approached the first waiting steelhead, the fly pulled away toward midstream.

"Wade out right into the middle. There, that's it. Now cast! Now feed the slack out to them. Feed it right down their throats."

I let the loose line slip through the guides, careful not to jerk the rod tip. The fly sank deeper into the slot, the steelhead remained unimpressed.

"Move over," commanded Corsmo. "It's time to put a fish on the beach."

He waded into the flow and made a smart roll cast that lined the bend perfectly. Instantly three small steelhead disappeared in beams of their own light.

"What the hell was that all about?" Corsmo demanded. But I felt much better knowing that the gods still rewarded hubris in the usual manner.

We followed the river's fluid meander downstream until we came upon a slick pool. Its deep side was enveloped in forest shadow as dark and full of detail as a Rembrandt. Corsmo gazed into the black pool as if it were a sacred reliquary. He allowed me the honor of passing through it first. I stood at the thin edge of the shadow and cast. My backcast passed behind me through the border of sunlight and rolled out before me into shadow.

Halfway down the pool, I came suddenly upon a small steelhead of about only two pounds. It didn't become airborne and it wasn't a fair fight on the big rod, but its sides were bright and fine and the fish had a lot of heart. I led it out of the pool and into the sunlit shallows, pausing to admire its silver and rose iridescence before letting it go.

It was Corsmo's turn. He waded into the current holding his rod aloft, no doubt hand-planed from the True Cross. At the tailout, the rod bent deeply into the cork and a magnificent steelhead vaulted into the air. It looked to be about ten pounds: not a trophy, but one truly noble fish nonetheless. Corsmo's line made a lovely, shearing sound as it sliced through the pool. The rod bent and recovered deeply. The fish bolted for the deepest lie.

Corsmo played the fish the way he shot pool—with his balls, his manhood—with muscle instead of finesse. Suddenly his rod lost its tension and I knew instantly the fish had broken off. There are hardly any words for this sort of tragicomedy, not even in Boontling.

Corsmo dragged himself out of the pool. To his credit, he laughed and said, "I need a drink."

We fished on down the river, taking turns at the pools. Corsmo landed two small steelhead known locally as "half pounders," and I landed none. We hauled ourselves up the bank sometime in late afternoon and sat for a while in the sun. The light in the redwoods made me think of Grace Cathedral in San Francisco. I knew full well this tract along the river had been spared the buzz saw so the tourists wouldn't scream bloody murder. Corsmo must have read my mind. "I wouldn't take the whole of Louisiana Pacific," he said, "for a single molecule of water in this river."

We drove to the Pacific Ocean to watch the breakers crash against the headlands as if in a Robin-

Hot Creek

We followed flashes of dry lightning down into the desiccated caldera of the Owens Valley, where the mainly treeless eastern slope of the Sierra drops suddenly into tan and endless space and the sagebrush hills more closely resemble Wyoming than they do California. Here the rivers spill and disappear into the desert bottoms or the shining wastes of Nevada.

The arid basin of the Owens once was a lush valley of cattle ranches, orchards and wheat farms. But that was before Los Angeles, roughly two hundred and fifty miles away, decided to steal the water and suck this remote Eden dry. That was in the early twenties, when Los Angeles Water and Power clandestinely bought up and incorporated most of the river-bottom land and rights-of-way along the river in order to secretly irrigate crops in the San Fernando Valley and ultimately expand the metropolis. This huge rip-off of the Owens ranchers eventually became a part of the mythology of the West, where Mark Twain had earlier observed that whisky was for drinking, water for fighting over. The Owens deception also served as the inspiration for the film *Chinatown*, the *Citizen Kane* of detective movies. "You see, Mr. Gitts," John Huston's villain explains to private eye Jack Nicholson in the film's dramatic climax, "either you bring the water to L.A., or you bring L.A. to the water."

L.A. still comes to the water, but now it's to fish Hot Creek, the most carefully picked-over stream in California. Hot Creek is a tributary of the Owens River and roughly equidistant from both L.A. and my home in San Francisco. But L.A rightly has dibs on this priceless spring creek. You see, it's the nearest decent trout fishing for any angler unlucky enough to be living in the City of Angels.

"The history of Southern California," said my friend Hal, "is nothing less than an accounting of its lost possibilities."

He spoke with the smugness all San Franciscans affect when commenting on the Southland. Here it was again: The Speech. Southern California once was a paradise of ocean, desert and free-wheeling condors, where steelhead boldly swam up Malibu Creek. Whoa. Before Hal could launch into his tirade against Walt Disney and the Magic Kingdom, his right foot suddenly smashed down onto the brake of his pickup, sending the rear end of the vehicle into a series of fishtailing cosines. A jackrabbit peeled off Highway 395 unharmed.

"I hear it's good luck to hit those things," he muttered.

"Only in Reno, Hal."

It was late afternoon and the mountain shadows were absorbing the ultraviolet light. The black thunderheads had fled south toward Bishop. Hal insisted we first fish the sweeping meadow of the upper Owens River where presumably the wind wouldn't be as bad as in Hot Creek Canyon. Hal presumed wrong. The wind made the fence wires around us vibrate like plucked harpstrings and we struggled to form our casts into wind-cheating bows.

I waded into the water and felt the motion of the river slowly leave me for Lone Pine and the high desert. The lower Owens is a lost cause, siphoned off to fill the swimming pools of L.A. Well to the south, the twenty-mile-long dry bed of Owens Lake gleams like a bleached bone at the foot of the Panamints. But the upper Owens where we stood is a fly fisherman's dreamscape, one of the region's few true spring creeks. Its valley floor sits seven thousand feet above sea level in a zone of clear spring-fed headwater and perfect trout habitat. It may be the best place to stand and view the eastern wall of California. From the valley, the Sierras rise up against the sky like galleons.

The river wound languorously through the meadow; mayflies hatched and floated toward the sun. I drifted a caddis imitation over a deep cutbank and intercepted a big rainbow on its way up-stream to deliver a genetic message sent an eon ago. In spring, rainbows pour out of the huge down-stream impoundment of Crowley Lake to spawn. In autumn, the browns there feel the planet's pivotal tug and stream upriver just about the time mallards get the urge to rocket out of the ponds and pot-holes, climb to three thousand feet and point their green heads toward Mexico.

The east slope of the Sierras provides a banquet for fishermen and among anglers you will hear inevitable arguments over whether the best brown trout fishing in California is to be found in the Owens watershed or in the East Walker River just a little farther north. The case in favor of the East Walker appears largely historical now, thanks to a severe drawdown of the Bridgeport Reservoir that buried the river's spawning gravel in enough silt to fill the Astrodome. Lawsuits were filed and lawyers summoned, bearing their load of inertia. This is California, after all. Environmentalists predict a big comeback for the East Walker but Hal is not convinced. "You might as well tag the toe and close the drawer," he said.

My friend is a notorious fly-fishing misanthrope. He once showed me a scornful letter he wrote to the owners of an aquatic amusement park with the bewildering name of Marine World Africa, USA, in Vallejo, just north of San Francisco, proposing an enterprise he called "Tarpon Rodeo." Performers would ride bucking tarpon and rodeo clowns would run out and collapse into the pools to distract the giant herring. Hal assured Marine World that his idea would be more profitable than a Ponzi scheme because, as everyone knows, rodeo performers, like circus folk, "are the lowest-paid people in show business." Marine World's response, if any, was not immediately forthcoming.

Come evening, the wind stopped sweeping down the draws. We found the trunk road that leads to Hot Creek where the stream winds through a small canyon of lava outcroppings. From this narrow defile the view upstream is unmatched. The upper creek makes serpentine cuts through a stark western meadow and beyond it rise sagebrush hills and finally the black peaks of the Sierras rimed in snow. I counted nine rustic A-frames on the meadow, the housekeeping cabins of Hot Creek Ranch. Only paying guests get to fish this stretch of open meadow. Everybody else must make do with the canyon water.

The creek here is pretty much the same as upstream: identical meadow features with a few riffles thrown in as the water gushes over cold stones and pea gravel. Underwater chara blooms and braids the currents, making long, casual drifts of the fly impossible. This calls for some of the trickiest fishing in America.

And from the look of it, this is some of the country's most intensely fished water. Fly fishermen lined up like SWAT teams along both banks of the canyon. Despite its desirability, or maybe because of it, very little of Hot Creek is actually open to the public. The canyon stretch is brief, flowing for less than a mile before hitting the warm underground discharge that gives the creek its name. The smelly, sulfurous pool that forms here makes for world-class skinny-dipping, but creates a permanent thermal barrier to the fish, blocking downstream migration to the Owens and Crowley Lake. These hot springs are here because the whole area is sunk into a huge volcanic caldera rigged with trip-wire fault lines that set off daily harmonic temblors, most too slight to actually be detected except by sensitive seismic instruments in Berkeley and Palo Alto.

There's a lot more casting room on Hot Creek Ranch if you've got the cash for a cabin. This is where the legends started, after all. This two-mile private meadow stretch is the only water in America actually restricted to fishing with dry flies, if you can believe it. Sort of like a British chalk stream with rattlesnakes. It's as if Frederic Halford had wandered confused into a Zane Grey sunset.

You're not even allowed to wade into the shallow creek for fear of crushing the delicate water plants. These effete rules were set down in 1910, when the ranch began charging anglers fifty cents a day for the privilege of casting over its huge brown trout. The dry-fly proviso was included in the covenant of sale when the ranch changed hands and remains inviolate to this day.

All these conservation measures might account for the fact that there are a staggering eleven thousand trout in every mile of this narrow little creek. Most of the Hot Creek fish are browns. The

Owens, which also has private catch-and-release fishing, on the Arcularius and Alpers ranches, holds similar numbers of fish, mostly rainbows. Little wonder half of Los Angeles joined us in the valley.

For once my friend didn't make any smart-ass remarks when he saw the other anglers on the stream. Instead he proceeded to fish Hot Creek with aplomb. Hal's line looped and whistled in the air like a singing wire.

Caddises drifted by on the surface in numbers too insignificant to inspire rises. It took me a while to make out the natural camouflage of the trout hunkering down by the chara beds. But there they were, holding themselves in the current, mysterious, lovely and dumb. How many mayfly imitations do they see drift past their snouts each season? Yet somehow they never learn. Directly below me an angler lined in a fish that had fallen to his feathered booby trap. I studied the bank water at my feet for long minutes before a brown trout, well over eighteen inches, suddenly materialized in the current's cold refraction. He had been there all along. My desire to possess him was almost infernal.

Soon trout began smutting on the surface, feeding sporadically. Above the creek, clouds of tiny mayflies mated, spinning like atoms in the final light. A small rainbow grabbed my fly and performed a few aerial turns before trying to cheat me in the weeds. I brought him quickly to hand.

Nighthawks wheeled in the dusk and shadows sifted through the canyon. My big German brown made a slow-motion rise and sipped in a bug. I tied on a small fly that might have been an olive emerger, it was really too dark to tell. I cast downstream and then fed slack line out my rod tip until the tiny fly passed over the feeding lane. I repeated this three more times before the big brown rose and struck.

The line sheared through the water, making a sound like a ripping bedsheet. The fish veered erratically beneath the surface and headed for the weedbeds, but I horsed him in anyway, only a cobweb-thin leader between us.

For some moments, I held the heavy fish in my hands to admire its gigantic black spots and scattered red moons. And then I slipped the fish back into Hot Creek.

It's times like these, on the hike back to the pickup truck, under the first faint starlight, that you wonder just what it is you have done right with your life to deserve such a gift.

Fool's Gold

The treasure which you think not worth taking trouble and pains to find, this one alone is the real treasure you are longing for all your life.

—B. Traven,
The Treasure of the Sierra Madre

I went up to fish the north fork of the Stanislaus River in the Sierra foothill country the day after Ellie Nesler changed her plea to innocent by reason of temporary insanity. The reporters had cleared out of the tiny Gold Rush town of Sonora, leaving only us tourists to clog its historic main street as we passed through on our way to the mountains. It seems that Ellie, a mother raising a young son on her own, was going to have to stand trial for murder. She had smuggled a handgun into the town's makeshift courtroom and shot the man who was accused of molesting her child. Ellie thought she saw the defendant smirk, so she administered "frontier justice," firing five bullets into the back of the man's head and neck. Reporters quickly descended on Sonora, treating the community as if it were a vigilante theme park, turning human tragedy into horse opera.

Of course, every tourist bureau and chamber of commerce in

every former mining town in the California gold country would have you believe that theirs was once the roughest, most lawless mining camp in the West. But they'd rather you not know that the Sierra foothill country today can still be a haven for lowlifes and social misfits. Public support for Ellie, very high at first, dropped off dramatically after it was made public that a medical examination conducted upon her arrest showed she had been high on crank at the time of the shooting. Welcome to the New West.

I was searching for other myths. Near Angels Camp, once a boomtown of saloons and brothels, I stopped in the middle of the causeway that spans New Melones Reservoir and gazed out at the expanse of flat blue water to the east. Fourteen years ago, an activist and river boatman by the name of Mark Dubois had chained himself to a rock in the Stanislaus River canyon and threatened to let himself be drowned if the canyon was filled. His heroic protest brought the flooding to a halt, albeit temporarily. Eventually New Melones Reservoir was filled, submerging a canyon that had taken the Stanislaus River nine million years to carve, and entombing what at the time was the most popular stretch of white-water rapids in California.

The road to the north fork climbed steadily from the foothills to five thousand feet above sea level. In the canyon below, the Stanislaus lay coiling over golden stones and its rapids split the sunlight. The water passed over black and golden rock in alternations of light and shadow. Although I couldn't hear the river from this height, I knew that deep in the canyon it would be roaring.

I drove into Calaveras Big Trees Park under the green and solemn shadows of sequoias and ponderosa pines. My destination was Beaver Creek. I wanted to slip a few casts into that stream before trying the bigger water. Unlike the north fork, swollen and freezing with snowmelt from the distant Sierra peaks, chances were excellent that this tributary would be in optimum shape.

There was only one thing wrong with this cold, slightly acidic creek where I made my first casts. The small rainbows rose easily to my dry fly, but their pink bands and olive bodies were faded, as if someone had left a fine oil painting out in the sun. These were planters. I'd have to bushwhack well upstream to get to any wild trout. Perhaps I should have gone one mountain over to the south, to Griswold Creek, which is never seeded. Because of the steep terrain, access is limited and often tough in this country. The hatchery trucks unload at the few easy "put-ins." Unless I was willing to leg it, I would be fishing to a lot of faded masterpieces.

I scrambled down the creek path for a half-mile, hoping to get into some brook trout that the creek is said to harbor. I love the sleek little American char. A favorite poet, the late Dick Hugo, once said of the sides of a char that "its orange spots flare like far-off fires." A friend of the poet once noted that as far as Hugo was concerned—Alexander Pope notwithstanding—the proper study of mankind was fish. Come to think of it, Hugo was strictly a bait-and-spin fisherman. No flies on this poet. He liked good saloons, too. He said of a bar in Dixon, Montana, that on a bad day you could drink until you were the mayor. But there were no brook trout waiting for me in the glittering riffles and narrow fissures of this creek. Only more diminished hatchery fish. Time to climb out and head for the big water.

For some reason, the western slope of the Sierra Nevada enjoys a somewhat indifferent fishing reputation. The conventional wisdom is that the rivers there—only three hours from San Francisco, scarred by gold dredges and plundered by hydroelectric pirates—hold few big fish and are best passed over for more mythical waters on the other side of the Range of Light or in the volcano country up around Shasta. Yet, like much conventional wisdom, I suspect it is wrong. Looking out at the brawling north fork of the Stanislaus smashing down out of these mountains in spring torrent, and contemplating the remoteness and beauty of its largely inaccessible canyon, I could only believe that these rivers held monsters.

On a dirt road near Sourgrass Crossing, a speeding logging truck sprayed my car with gravel. Looking back I saw that the load of shorn timber it carried was made up of young sequoias, not the smaller, more common ponderosa. The desire to reach like Ellie Nesler for a handgun and administer a little frontier justice of my own was nearly irresistible. Louisiana Pacific Lumber logs heavily in these hills.

The gate one mile down from this dirt road is kept locked in the off-season to keep people from stealing firewood out of the forest. Well, people have been looting these canyons in one way or another ever since James Marshall discovered gold at Sutter's Mill on the American River in January, 1848. Within a year the stampede was on to the Mother Lode, the 120-mile-long primary deposit of gold ore that runs—or, rather, ran before the vein played out—north to south from Auburn at the forks of the American to Melones on the Stanislaus.

The west slope river canyons, which are nothing less than great vertical cracks in the Sierra wall, only look as if they're in a natural, wild state today. The scars of the Gold Rush are everywhere in the foothills. Greedy miners stripped the canyon land and flushed the soil out to sea. What the forty-niners couldn't pan or dredge out of the rivers, they dug out from the rock wall. And what they couldn't mine, they hosed down from the hillsides with powerful water jets that burst the earth, shooting the runoff into sluice boxes that retained the heavier gold. Fields of boulders from this hydraulic mining line the riverbanks today.

The great enduring irony of the Gold Rush was that few miners actually got rich, leaving the real windfalls to entrepreneurs like William Knight, who raked in five hundred dollars a day ferrying miners across the Stanislaus. The truly big killings were made by canny speculators and cutthroat businessmen, like the merchants who sold the miners eggs for three bucks apiece or a fifth of rotgut whiskey for sixteen dollars. Like so many of the dreamers, James Marshall, the man who discovered gold at Sutter's Mill, went bust in the end, reduced in his final days to selling his autograph. Not the vendors. An obscure San Francisco merchant named Levi Strauss was one who did well for himself making durable blue work pants for the men in the gold fields. His company's logo rides high on my backside.

Modern prospectors still dredge these rivers, their fingers itching. But the real gold is now the water itself, and California's effort to harness it—for irrigation, hydroelectric power and flood control—has left changes even more profound than those wrought by the Gold Rush.

The filling of New Melones Reservoir in 1983 did more than drown upwards of six hundred archaeological and anthropological sites in the canyon and kill a world-class stretch of rapids that attracted fifty thousand rafters and kayakers each year (the second most popular run of white water in America). The flooding ended a bitter and monumental battle between the powerful water lobbies and river activists, and sent to the ballot box the country's only statewide initiative to stop a dam. The water developers outspent the conservationists and through misleading advertising ("Save the river, vote no") gulled California's voters into believing that the dam was actually a conservation project. New Melones Reservoir began filling from the north, middle and south forks in 1979 and gradually, over three years, the water rose inexorably, drowning forever such legendary rapids as Chinese Dogleg, Parrotts Ferry, Rock Garden, Devil's Staircase and Mother Rapid.

I hiked down into the north fork canyon a mile above Sourgrass Crossing. White noise coming through the trees left the forest birds mute. The river came as a great surprise anyway. I stepped suddenly out of the pines to find myself standing at the final chute of a fierce rapid, its plume spraying and blowing away. Below this the river seemed to bend with great force and gather itself into a cold green chamber of oxygen and refracted light.

I tied on a large dry and flicked it across the surface transparency, wanting it to disappear in the blink of a rise. The turbulence felt numb with snowmelt; I could feel the north fork against my legs, straining for the Central Valley. I switched to a heavily weighted stone-fly nymph, lobbed it like a stone upstream, stack-mended line to get the proper sink and dredged the bottom like a forty-niner.

Because of their great vertical drop, these rivers scour their beds clean, leaving little for plant and insect life to cling to. Thus their reputation for small, widely scattered trout. But I have talked to men who fish these waters frequently, men who live down below in the valley, who tell of twenty-inch trout holding steady in the current as if in ether, ten feet beneath the surface, behind shadowy, golden boulders.

Standing at the edge, rolling out great loops of line, I thought of the permits that had been taken out by developers, then hastily withdrawn, for a multimillion-dollar hydroelectric project that would have placed diversionary dams directly above Calaveras Big Trees Park where I was now fishing. There is talk about giving the north fork "wild and scenic" status.

My line looped far out over the rushing river. I quartered the fly downstream and came up on a solid take. It was a decent fish, hard fighting, full of the life of the river and, with the current propelling it, just strong enough to pull one short protest from my clicking Hardy. I eased the fish out into the shallows and admired the faintly lavender-and-pink cast of a stream-bred rainbow trout. The caudal fin and flaring violet gill plate seemed almost transparent, as if allowing light to pass through before diffusing it. I held the trout in the current. Flecks of iron pyrite glittered in the gravel and cobbled channel.

Above, hawks whistled at the cliffs and rode the thermals skyward. I was alone in a deep canyon with a great roaring river to fish. All that afternoon, trout flashed messages to me in the dark current, in the airy foam.

The trick lies in knowing what is being said.

The Canyon No One Knows

It was a hot morning in late June and we'd descended into the canyon to the put-in to find that the river was at high water, higher than it had been for seven summers, and rising. California's long drought was over. A white tympanic sound filled the air.

I was here as a guest of the Tuolumne River Preservation Trust. I had never been white-water rafting before and the Tuolumne River ranked among the more fearsome runs. Still, I wanted to explore a side canyon on a tributary called the Clavey, which had been threatened with a proposed hydroelectric project. Everyone in our group was either a professional conservationist or a river guide except me. Near as I could tell, I had been invited along in the capacity of official "trout poet."

The Clavey is one of the last remaining streams on the western slope of the Sierra Nevada range whose natural habitat is relatively intact. There's a strain of rainbow trout in the Clavey that has been here since before the Spaniards set foot in the New World. They make up one of the last pure strains of the original rainbow trout once found in California. I was going to risk drowning to see this river, and I hadn't even brought along a rod. I badly wanted to see the stream that the American

Rivers Foundation in Washington, D.C., had just named one of the ten most endangered rivers in America.

Our guides, Chris Condon and Chris Jonason, both of Sierra Mac River Trips in Sonora, gathered at the bank, as if looking for a sign. There was a general stirring and murmuring around the put-in and an air of mock concern and gallows humor. My mouth was out of spit. Less than one hundred yards downstream from the put-in, the faintly green Tuolumne boiled and foamed white at the first rapid. The rapids come suddenly on this river, one right after another, with little slow water in between.

"If you fall out," said Chris Condon, "and can't get back into the raft, grab a rock or make for the bank. If you don't get out in time, you'll be swept down into the next rapid."

Wiry, lean and bearded, he spoke with the cheerful authority of a seasoned river rat. I noticed that our second guide, Chris Two as we called her, had a small butterfly tattooed on her tan shoulder.

We listened intently to Condon, even though I was the only one who hadn't heard the lecture before.

"Can you breathe?" Condon asked me, tugging on the side straps of my flotation vest.

"Yes," I said.

"Then it isn't tight enough," he said, giving the straps a ferocious yank.

We launched the two rafts and, before I knew it, the first rapid was sucking us toward its sudden rush. The river accelerated and we moved toward a wall of scissoring waves. On a river, unlike the ocean, it is the water that moves; the waves stay in place.

son Jeffers poem. *I'd sooner, except the penalties, kill a man than a hawk.* Jeffers was obviously our country's last clear-thinking poet.

We headed back for San Francisco. In Boonville, I stopped at the Buckhorn Saloon to buy Corsmo a bottle of the locally brewed beer. The circumstances seemed to call for it.

The saloon, built in 1873, was filled with the usual mixture of Valley rednecks and burned-out counterculturists who fled to Mendocino in the sixties. Corsmo gazed into his glass as if he might find his steelhead in it.

He took a polite sip, lost in the rivers of his youth. "It's all changed," he said. "I keep telling myself I won't bother, and every winter I come back."

It's a familiar refrain. People are always complaining that things aren't what they used to be. In San Francisco, they play this broken record more than Tony Bennett. Which doesn't make it any the less true. We talked about all the rivers in our lives and for a while we let their memory wash over us. I thought Corsmo might get puling drunk. But he seemed oddly content. As we rose to leave, I noticed his beer was hardly touched. A day on the river will do that to a man.

When we got back to the city, the moon was high over the TransAmerica Building, and the Golden Gate Bridge seemed a ghostly span. Out beyond the straits, the Pacific rolled and surged. Like Henry Corsmo, the steelhead were coming home, too.

Hat Creek

Truly it can be said (as Samuel Johnson said of London) that he who has tired of the City by the Bay, has tired of life. By late April I was.

The downtown was even crazier than usual, more homeless than ever were milling hopelessly about, and the streets looked less like the tourist brochures than they did the outtakes from *Blade Runner*. A day's drive away were deserts, mountains, redwood forests, spectacular coastlines and trout streams. I planned to be on one, Hat Creek. Hat is celebrated: an incredibly nutrient-rich spring creek that percolates up from lava fields surrounding Lassen National Forest, and on whose surface the mayflies rise and scatter in sparkling transparency. I suggested Hat Creek for the season's opener.

"Good idea," snorted my friend Hal. "After all, California has some of the world's finest second-rate trout fishing."

Which is not exactly the way the Chamber of Commerce might have put it. Hal, a lifelong San Franciscan, usually spends the opening week of the season fishing not for trout, but for a rare and little-publicized run of summer steelhead that ascends the middle fork of the Eel River. While everyone is out hammering the trout streams senseless, Hal has an entire steelhead highway to himself. "Don't go to Hat on the weekend," Hal warned me. "There'll be more anglers there than caddis flies."

It was Hal who taught me the rivers of California when I first moved here and although we have been friends for several years, there is always an undercurrent of tension between us. Perhaps it is because I am yet one more out-of-state migrant crowding his rivers. Or perhaps it's because I once referred to him in print as the Antichrist of fly fishing.

The following Sunday Hal called me to say he was canceling his Eel River trip. I wasn't surprised. The Lost Coast up there had been stunned over the weekend by a devastating earthquake and was still radiating aftershocks like a tuning fork. The middle Eel was comfortably out of range of the epicenter, but Hal wanted no part of it, anyway. For a native Californian, he is a remarkable sissy when it comes to earthquakes and keeps water jugs and other survival provisions at the ready in his North Beach apartment. His TV set is lashed down with Velcro, which I maintain is taking things too far. On the other hand, I prepare for the likelihood of a seismic cataclysm in the manner of most of my fellow Californians, which is to say I refuse to consider it at all.

"Are you still going up to the Hat?" Hal asked me over the telephone. When I told him I was, Hal said he would come too. His tone seemed to imply we would both regret it. Knowing Hal, someone probably had once crossed his line on the Hat and he never went back.

Trout fishing in the Golden State, I'd discovered, can be a questionable series of trade-offs. It's best not to believe everything you hear or read, particularly in what my friend likes to call "the trout porno magazines." I remember my first experience with Putah Creek, a dam-release stream that flows out of Lake Berryessa. Everybody had been touting it as the best-moving trout water nearest San Francisco. I even found references to Putah Creek in Ernest Schwiebert's sprawling, two-volume *Trout*. Schwiebert favorably compares Putah Creek's aquatic weedbeds and rich insect life with Hat Creek and even refers to it, perhaps in jest, as a "wine-country chalk stream." What the creek reminded me of was not so much a chalk-stream idyll as a battery-acid spill. The water, a corrosive bluish green, flowed from the dam with a turbidity that left the creek opaque. You couldn't judge its depths well enough to see where to plant your wading boots. True, Putah Creek held big rainbow trout that migrated upstream to spawn in February, but you fished for them in a ruined ambiance.

The next morning we drove north toward Redding, which sits in an inverted bowl at the top of the Sacramento Valley. Hemmed in by the Trinity-Salmon Alps and the Cascades, the citizens of Redding enjoy some of the hottest temperatures in California. Mount Shasta, California's highest mountain, its volcanic peak eternally covered in glacial snow, rises up in the distance like a monstrance.

We turned east out of the valley, which baked and shimmered, and ascended into the tall pines and cool mountain air of Lassen National Forest. Hat Creek is a tributary of the Pit River, and I asked Hal if we might try it. He said there were so many dams in the Pit's deep-fissure canyons that you practically had to have a degree in engineering to fish it. The Pit's flow is dramatic but unnatural, roaring out of a series of reservoirs and powerhouses. There it was again, that ambiance thing.

We took a motel room in the resort town of Burney and then drove to what is known as the trophy trout section of lower Hat Creek. We got to it by a steep utility road that led to the Hat No. 2 Powerhouse. The first thing I noticed were twelve electrical power lines stretched high above the creek's riffle section. They were buzzing like angry hornets.

Hal laughed harshly and said, "Why don't you see if one of those fly-fishing magazines wants to buy a story about someone who gets leukemia fishing under those things? You can call it 'Leuko-cytes and Strike Indicators.'" Here was social satire at its best.

There were only a few anglers on the creek, all fishing the easier riffle water under the power lines. Risking a fatal drop in my blood cell count, I waded into the riffles under the electrical field and promptly caught a modest but vivid rainbow trout on a little Bird's Nest nymph. It was the last trout I was to bring to hand that afternoon.

My friend chose to walk out into the meadow where the creek water flattens out. He continued downstream toward the beautiful and glassy slow water. Here, surely, was the most bewitching stretch of trout water in California. There is nothing quite so pleasing as a spring creek meandering through a western meadow. Hat, which rises from underground springs and has extremely high concentrations of bound carbon dioxide, is frequently compared to rivers like the Firehole in Wyoming and Silver Creek in Idaho, although I personally feel this is wishful thinking on somebody's part. Bubbling up through volcanic strata, the carbon dioxide dissolves vast limestone deposits, enriching the water with the kind of alkalinity that produces dense weed growth and abundant insect life. For just over two miles of this meadow section, much of the surface of Hat Creek is as clear and flat as windowpane. The water is so pure you can see right to the streambed and it is a delight just to be able to watch the mysterious weeds swaying in the current.

My friend stepped into this gloss and began casting. It is always a pleasure to watch the loft and timing of a truly great caster, particularly one who uses an old-fashioned bamboo rod. The long loops drifted and unfurled with deliberate, almost exaggerated slowness. Such casting seemed to leave behind an image of itself, like looking at a memory.

The big trout, rainbows and German browns were hiding by the weedbeds. The water was transparent and slick and wouldn't disguise mistakes. At the moment, there were no insects riding on the slowly moving glass of the creek. Angling writers have an in word for this kind of water: "technical," meaning, I suppose, that it has many different insect hatches coming off at the same time, or that it calls for perfect presentations on long invisible leaders. Maybe it just means tough—tricky. My friend must have done something extremely "technical," because there he was, suddenly bringing a struggling, deep-bodied trout to net.

Much has been written about the supposed intelligence of trout on these kinds of streams. One of our favorite conceits is to see ourselves playing a game of chess with them, Bobby Fischer rising dripping out of the Beaverkill to suggest an Alekhine's Defense or the Falkbeer Counter Gambit. Fact is, you could hide a trout's brain under a loose acorn cap. To say that one species of trout—a brown, for instance—is more intelligent than another is like calling Moe the smarter Stooge. Trout react to two things, danger and hunger, and not very well to either, judging from how easily they are caught and how easily they are duped into taking fake food.

Come evening, I wandered back upstream to the broken-riffle section where the creek poured out from the Pacific Gas and Electric Company powerhouse. I wanted to get below those riffles, to where the water flattened out but still had enough movement to hide a faulty presentation. Here I was told was the place to be for a caddis hatch that starts just before dark and quickly turns into a Roman orgy.

In the failed light, tiny caddises mated in irregular flight above the water. Big dive-bombing stone flies, too, a few dropping heavily onto the surface, but the trout wouldn't come up for them. And then gradually, the rings of rising trout began to appear as the greater biomass of the caddises began to alight on the creek. In the excitement, I felt the sudden loss of cabin pressure I experience in a rise and I had to will myself to slow down and aim the casts to the trout rings. I struck two fish, momentarily feeling their heaviness beneath my rod, but the fly popped loose both times. In just ten minutes, the much-vaunted caddis fall was over and the sky was dark. We drove back to Burney, fiddling with the car radio, trying to get a clear signal through the mountains.

Despite a forecast of rain, the following day arrived warm, fragrant and bright as a hummingbird's wings. I decided to explore the riffle section above the powerhouse. The creek was much narrower here, hemmed in by bushes, pines and scaly incense cedars. All along the bank, mayflies gathered in glittering swarms. They were Pale Morning Duns, early for the season, and I was particularly pleased to see my favorite western mayfly here. They have the loveliest of names and for my money are the last word in mayfly elegance. The tiny yellowish insects were just beginning their midmorning mating swarm. It would be a short while before the ovipositing females dropped their egg sacs on the water and the males fell to the surface, spent and delerious as teenage boys.

I crossed the creek, walked well down from the power lines and waded out to wait for the rises. Pretty soon insect specks drifted by in the film and the trout came up to sip politely. My fly disappeared in one of the rings. I lifted my rod and got a wake-up call from the creek. A brilliantly colored rainbow vaulted out of the water and bent my Granger into the butt. When I finally landed him, I could see he was at least fifteen inches long and had that solid, chunky feel so characteristic of a rainbow trout. I slipped out the barbless hook and eased the fish back into the current.

By afternoon it grew overcast and the wind kicked up, wrinkling the surface of the creek. I hiked downstream for at least two miles, past rolling bankside meadows and chalky bluffs. Blackbirds perching in the cattails flushed at my approach. Horses grazed behind ranch fences.

Beyond the valley are taller hills scattered with sage. The creek here hasn't been stocked in twenty years. All the trout from the powerhouse to the fish barrier at Britton Lake are wild. The farther you walk, the more remote it all seems. Hat begins with rain and snowmelt sliding off the north slope of Hat Peak in Lassen Park, taking its chances like any other freestone stream. But at Cassel, a mere dot on the map, it is transformed, picking up most of its flow from the lush spring heads of its tributary, Rising River. All of Rising River is private. Bing Crosby used to own much of the headwater property; now it's in Clint Eastwood's hands. I wondered momentarily what it might be like to poach on Dirty Harry's trout stream. Probably not a good idea. I had a sudden nightmare vision of all the trout rivers in California being given away on Oscar night. "I would like to thank the Academy for awarding me the East Walker River . . ."

By evening the wind had died, the clouds had scattered and we enjoyed a much greater caddis hatch than the night before. The fishing was absolutely narcotic. "Great evening," muttered my friend when it was over. In the dark, we broke down our rods and talked with the other departing fishermen who gathered in the clearing below the powerhouse where everyone parks their cars. But as usual, the conversation turned to who owned the most expensive tackle and who last booked the entire South Island of New Zealand for himself. This kind of talk grows stale fast, so Hal and I decided to take one last look at the meadow and the dark creek. You could hear the trout sipping something unseen out there in the black zones of the flat water. The country night was deep and the starlight clear. We headed home.

On Zane Grey's River

There are many beautiful rivers. This is the most beautiful. Chances are, you carry such a river around with you. But the one I am smitten with is the North Umpqua in Oregon. It is the most arresting river I ever stepped into. I am leery of using such superlatives. Yet no other river gives me this kind of joy. Zane Grey wrote about the Rogue, but he was downright possessive about the Umpqua.

There are no steamboats on the North Umpqua, nor have paddle wheelers ever plied this river. Yet here I was on the edge of the Station Hole casting once again to summer steelhead directly below a creek called Steamboat and just out of sight of the Steamboat Inn. The term as it is used here is a leftover from the last century and refers to a mining claim that "steamboated" or didn't pan out. And it seems to fit. I had been on the North Umpqua for two weeks trying to catch a steelhead. And it looked like I might be taking the steamboat out.

I came to the river by way of the Oregon desert, fishing the huge Deschutes. By day, the canyon was a blast furnace. But as the sun fell, the river cooled, the walls turned umber and the canyon transformed itself into a gallery of shadows. In a long riffle below Maupin, I banked an exquisite redside trout, but failed to come upon a steelhead.

Next morning I drove upriver past the lodgepole forest at Bend where the high desert meets the Cascades and then west into the mountains toward the cool plateau of Diamond Lake. The highway climbed steadily into a dense evergreen forest and the air tasted like spring water. Below Toketee Falls, I saw the river for the first time, a series of blue-green pools and spraying rapids rushing through a steep-walled canyon and over a bedrock of volcanic stone. Its still pools were tinged with grays and violets, mirroring towering stands of Douglas fir and Oregon sky.

The narrow, two-lane highway followed the river high above a fir-lined corridor to Steamboat Creek. Sixteen-wheeler logging rigs thundered past me on the way. There I stopped at Steamboat Inn, a landmark as famous as the river itself.

I walked around the inn proper, to the split-cedar cabins pitched in a half-moon above the river, almost hidden in a thick stand of sugar pines and Douglas firs. I stepped across the deck slats to the nearest railing and watched the river below fall in plumes of spray and gather in a green-chambered pool called the Glory Hole.

Inside the inn, a painting done in the violets and blues of the Umpqua showed mist rising out of a wine bottle to become river water and pines. A steelhead played in its ethereal currents. I passed a fieldstone fireplace and sat down at a vast table that had been planed from a single slab of sugar pine and salvaged from a legendary steelhead camp across the river. I gazed at the photographs on the walls of notable anglers who had fished the river, including the Big Daddy of them all, Zane Grey.

There were other, more recent photographs, too. Someone named Dan Callahan had opened his f-stops at the aperture of the river's soul. His Umpqua was full of deep-filtered light, colors you could drown in and river mist you could taste. I noticed that in one photograph, the fisherman in the background appeared to be Jack Hemingway. He had been fishing for steelhead at Steamboat in the fateful summer of 1961 when he learned that his father, Ernest Hemingway, had shot himself.

I asked some questions, bought some tackle and headed for the camp water. Just above Steamboat Creek, I crossed a rumbling steel-trestlework bridge that led to the U.S. Forest Service station on the south bank, the site of an old fishing camp once run by retired Major Lawrence Mott of the U.S. Army Signal Corps. There the Mott foot trail led through stands of fir, red cedar, thick-trunked sugar pines, vine maples and dense alders to a series of perfectly formed river pools. It is sometimes said of the North Umpqua that the eddies are as clearly defined as the links on a golf course, but I feel this misses the point entirely. There is nothing manicured or artificial about this river. When I stepped into the cold silk of the lower Boat Pool I felt the river's great power and weight slide by me.

The river flowed over a bedrock of dark basalt through ledge-rock channels cut by volcanic upheaval. To wade it, it was necessary to walk out on precarious ledge rock polished smooth by an endless glissade of water. All that stuff about the river's slippery footing is no joke. The North Umpqua gives you religion. Even good waders have drowned here. The course is steep, the current unrelenting, the rocks covered in algal slime. This river takes no prisoners.

I struggled for purchase on a submerged ridge and saw my first steelhead finning below in the river's cold, refractive light. Soon I spotted other silvery gray shapes holding inside the shining current alongside ledges and shelves and sunken boulders.

There are twenty-six individual pools in the Steamboat area and I fished each one of them with something approaching complete absorption. They all had formal names—Surveyor, Hayden's Run and the Fighting Pool—and like good Hollywood character actors, each had its own quirky signature personality. Sawtooth, for instance, is named for a jagged reef that could cut an angler's line.

The three Mott pools honor Major Mott, who started the rough tent camp at Steamboat on land leased from the Forest Service. There is a photograph of the major hanging on the wall in the present Steamboat Inn that was taken in 1930, the year before Mott's death from cancer, showing him standing at parade rest with a thin bamboo fly rod in one hand and an immense Chinook salmon in the other that he had just plucked out of the Kitchen Pool.

The Ledge Pool is said to have been named by none other than Zane Grey. Upper and Lower Takahashi were named after George Takahashi, Grey's Japanese field cook. It was a tough little pool to fish. Takahashi gets the credit for making the pool accessible in the first place. It was he who chopped down the underbrush so Zane Grey could get to it. I took my first dunking there.

Whenever Grey went fishing, he did so on a grand, expeditionary scale. He used his considerable book royalties to finance fishing trips that were imperial in their extravagance. While his love of fishing was undeniable, one has to wonder if he ever truly made peace with the sport or the river he loved. Grey's contribution to angling—particularly big-game fishing—was enormous, but there was something empty in it, too. If the stories are true, few on the river even liked the man. Truth is, I never cared for his hyperthyroid prose either—not the angling stories and certainly not the horse operas.

Although the Rogue got most of the attention in Zane Grey's fishing stories, it was the Umpqua that he truly loved. Grey first came to the river in 1932 and was so impressed he returned each year afterward to fish out the summers. Grey demanded star treatment on his expeditions and even hired local thugs to guard his favorite pools. These stories, while hugely entertaining, may be apocryphal; his son, Loren Grey, who accompanied his father on these Umpqua trips, has flatly denied anything like this ever happened. But the author could be terribly condescending. In his preface to the only story he ever wrote about the Umpqua, Grey in effect described the people of Oregon as a bunch of hill apes incapable of appreciating or safeguarding their own river. Needless to say, he did not endear himself to the locals.

More revealing perhaps was Grey's treatment of George Takahashi. The camp cook appears as a comic foil in a number of the author's fishing stories. It isn't pretty. Grey poked broad comic fun at Takahashi's diminutive physical stature and tortured English syntax. You could get away with that back in 1932, but today it all feels uncomfortably racist. On the Umpqua, it was said that Grey was always relegating Takahashi to fish the lesser pools while he chose the prime spots. But legend has it that Takahashi was the better steelhead fisherman. Certainly he was the better liked. Two pools are named in his honor. Appropriately, no one seems to have bothered naming any of the pools after the world's best-selling author of Westerns.

At the Bridge Pool where I stood, a half-dozen steelhead hung suspended along a ledge in a bath of green light. Surface patterns shimmered teasingly, throwing black spots on the rocks below.

For eight straight days, I fished the river on an almost transcendental plane. I joined anglers on the high north bank to "glass" the river with binoculars. I fished every pool I could reach on the thirty-four-mile twisting ribbon of fly-only water. I lost myself in the commanding vistas of its canyons and forests. In the deep pool at Wright Creek, I mended line to sink the fly and nose it past boulders where steelhead hid. I skated dries over the dark surface of Surveyor Pool in the first shade of midafternoon, and in the run below Apple Creek I saw the huge bulge of a steelhead rise to my fly and miss. I fished the Ledges, the Honey Riffles and the Salmon Racks, and got no surrenders. In the camp waters, I saw fish taken out of the river so alive and wet their colors seemed to pour back into the water.

At Williams Creek, I hooked and lost a small steelhead. It was in 1937, while camped here, that Grey had suffered the crippling stroke that eventually killed him. He was dozing in a lounge chair under a hot sun after a morning of fishing. His son Romer took him to the hospital in Roseburg and from there he was transported by ambulance back to his home in Altadena in southern California. He never fully recovered from his partial paralysis and died two years later.

Zane Grey's ferocious battles with other anglers over the quest for world records—his megalomania, his shameless self-promotion—have been written about by others and need not be catalogued here. It's enough to know that his competitive streak was so poisonous it destroyed his great friendship with Fred Burnham, the superlative steelhead angler who taught Grey how to fish for sea-run rainbows on the Rogue River. Their relationship disintegrated during a blue-water trip for billfish off New Zealand when Burnham caught a record marlin and Grey, possibly fearing a challenge to his own world record, ignored Burnham's request to call in the catch.

And yet the man had passion. Certainly, he paid the price for being, or having been, Zane Grey. And I could understand—as I looked out at what he once described as his singing river, and at the forest spread out before me in a dozen shades of summer green—how he came to love this river above all others. One would be fortunate to spend his last day here.

It happened on Surveyor Pool. I was skating a dry fly across. As if watching a movie in which I had somehow unaccountably landed a minor, supporting role, I saw a steelhead rise to the surface and engulf the fly. My rod bent deeply and I felt a great heaviness move away from me underwater. Ten minutes we battled. And then I held the big steelhead in my arms. Its sides, a watery silver and rose, seemed to drain back into the river. The Umpqua flowed past with joy. I carefully released the great fish. The steelhead paused in the current for a brief moment, unsure, then shot suddenly away, disappearing into memory.

A deep and toneless vibration rose up all around us. Spray hung in the air, forming rainbows and sun-shot coronas of mist. Our raft quaked and dropped into a hole in the curling foam. Condon punched the raft through the standing backwave. The Tuolumne River smashed down on us from all sides.

We dove and rose and fell again over hills and valleys of water. The raft trembled over the ridge lines of the waves and heaved into the washout.

As promised, the rapids came up swiftly, bigger ones waiting for us around each bend, the banks wheeling away behind us. We came out of the one known as Frame Crusher—a Class IV rapid at this high stage—and the river slowed and turned to black-green glass. We drifted cautiously over this quiet floodwater toward the side canyon where the Clavey River poured into the bigger Tuolumne. Below this deceptive calm lay Clavey Falls, the preeminent rapid on the Tuolumne. Here the smooth surge of main current poured into the heart of a maelstrom, the river crashing upon the rubble of rock that fanned out from the mouth of Clavey Canyon. Soon we would shoot this torrent, one of the truly formidable white-water drops.

Our raft touched the bank and we scrambled out onto the stones to watch the ferocious chutes of Clavey Falls thundering and blowing away, as if implying a rush to mortality.

We embarked on foot into Clavey Canyon, Condon leading the way. For our group, there would be no white-water rafting on this tributary. The grade of the Clavey River is so steep and its plume of water so strong that only world-class kayakers and rafters have been able to descend its awesome Class V and VI rapids. It has been run fewer than twenty times.

We scrambled upstream over boulders and waded into clear pools and enjoyed the small, glistening waterfalls. Chris drew us to a rare limestone outcropping from the age of the dinosaurs—rare in this canyon of polished granite and schist—and pointed out a few of its porous features. I plucked the dried husk of a stone fly off the huge chunk of calcium and looked up at the gorge, a mass of steep cliffs and huge rounded boulders cut out of the metasedimentary rock. I tried to imagine the 413-foot dam that would plug this beautiful river upstream. I tried to picture in my mind's eye the powerhouse, the three diversion dams, eleven miles of tunnel, two miles of pipeline and the tangle of transmission lines and roads that would forever scar the canyon. Building a hydroelectric dam here would be like burning the *Mona Lisa* to cook a can of Spam.

The Clavey, fed by a rush of snowmelt and underground springs, begins high in the Emigrant Wilderness west of Yosemite National Park. It twists through ancient forests, high meadows and the largest stand of quaking aspen in the southern half of the Sierra Nevada range. The aspens, their white trunks virginal against the dark conifers, tremble at the slightest movement of air. The sound is a little like that made by a minor waterfall. In spring, the fine leaves, pale green and luminous, shimmer with the quality of underwater light. In autumn, the treetops glow like chandeliers.

As it gathers momentum, the river flows through Stanislaus National Forest, plunging through pitched canyons of scrub and digger pines, where hawks rise and disappear into the blue of the sky. The tawny slopes of the mountains are the color of a mountain lion's hide. A few of the big cats come down into the canyon in winter, interested, no doubt, in Yosemite's wandering deer herd. Bald and golden eagles nest here. This is home for the rare Sierra Nevada red fox and snowshoe hare, the tri-colored blackbird and limestone salamander and the lovely, graceful Tuolumne fawn lily, which grows no place else on earth except in the two canyons of the Tuolumne and Clavey Rivers.

"Trout fishermen tell me they love this river," said Johanna Thomas, who had just climbed drip-ping out of an icy river pool where I had been looking for the bronze flashes of trout. It was one hun-dred degrees in the canyon.

"Some of the fishermen don't want us to talk the river up," she said. Johanna and her group, the Tuolumne River Preservation Trust, want Congress to recognize the Clavey for the national treasure it is and bring it into the Wild and Scenic River System, removing it forever from the grasp of developers.

Actually, I knew that only a handful of renegade fly fishermen made the effort each season to hike down through the heat and rattlesnakes to cast their flies at this shimmering river. The canyon's too tough and has too few footpaths: it is almost inaccessible. But for those who do make the trek, the rewards are virtual solitude and trout with side colorings to die for.

They had better fish it while they can. The dam proposed will drown 2.8 miles of river. A pair of reservoirs will reduce to a trickle fully nineteen miles of the river in between the impoundments and the hydroelectric structures will most probably wipe out the wild trout fishery.

In 1971, at the urging of the conservation group California Trout, the state's Fish & Game Com-mission had declared the Clavey one of a handful of streams to be designated an official "wild trout" river. This had precluded hatchery plantings or the introduction of exotic species that would have corrupted the gene pool of the rainbows. It also meant that wilderness managers were encouraged to leave the surrounding landscape undisturbed. Yet now, more than twenty years later, the Clavey was in trouble. California's first "wild trout" river was threatened by developers coveting all the kinetic energy of the tumultuous Clavey. Only forty-eight miles long, the river drops a stunning seven thousand feet from its headwaters in the high Sierra to its interdiction point with the Tuolumne. The Clavey is the largest undammed tributary on the Tuolumne River and one of the last not already tamed by a hydro project. Those who back the dam—the Turlock Irrigation District in wealthy Turlock County in the Central Valley—insist that the Clavey River is their concession prize. They view it as the trade-off in a bitter battle that was waged to save the Tuolumne River a decade ago. When Congress brought the Tuolumne Canyon section below Yosemite (where we had been rafting) into the Wild and Scenic River System in 1984, the Clavey was purposely left out. This was interpreted by the pro-dam community to mean that Congress intended the Clavey to be developed under normal regulatory processes. The conservationists claim, however, that no such bargain was ever struck.

"Clavey Falls is the heart of the Tuolumne," said Joe Daly, who is president of the Tuolumne River Preservation Trust. He was accompanying us on our amble up the canyon. We had scrambled up the scree of a small cliff and were looking down into a staircase of cascading waterfalls and white plunge pools when Daly told me that at the height of the spring runoff, the huge "spike" or surge of water pouring into the Tuolumne can be greater than three thousand cubic feet per second. If the dam goes up, the controlled releases will range from a mere twenty cubic feet per second at its lowest ebb to only four hundred cubic feet at its highest flow. "The natural cycle of having a huge spring surge will be gone," said Daly.

We returned to the mouth of the canyon and assembled the rafts for the run down Clavey Falls, then maneuvered ourselves into the main current of the Tuolumne River, our two guides backrowing to hold the rafts in place as they eyed the tremendous rapid roaring in front of us.

A chorus of rebel yells shot up from our rafts and bounced off the rock walls as we drifted slowness toward the truly frightening torrent. Not a true waterfall, Clavey Falls on this day was a Class V rapid. The only higher designation was Class VI—impassable.

The rapid is a huge presence in the mind of every boatman on the river. They use only three terms to describe the Tuolumne: before Clavey, Clavey and after Clavey.

A roaring filled the air. I was so frightened, I felt as if I were being wheeled into surgery on a gurney.

Clavey Falls sucked us in. Standing waves drenched us. We paddled furiously, our oarsman, Chris Condon, shouting commands. If we lost momentum we would flip. The river boiled over boulders and rocks.

Big waves form in the holes that a river creates behind rocks and ledges. These holes can suck down boats and bodies and hold them under until the whirlpool decides to spit them out. They call these holes "keepers." Whenever the backwave of a hole is higher than your raft, you must line it up perfectly straight and punch through or be prepared to have the whole world turn upside down and white.

Before us a huge keeper opened in the river on our left. This was the most feared hole on the Tuolumne and to me it looked like a lunar crater. This is where rafts are devoured. A photographer friend, Val Atkinson, had wiped out here on his first run down the Tuolumne many years ago. He spent so much time on the bottom staring at fish that he doubted the hole would ever spit him out. Ever since then, he gets out and walks around Clavey Falls on the pretext of photographing rafts coming down.

Chris swung us toward the crater and, as they say in boatman's parlance, we kissed the right edge. The raft slid down over the lip into a portion of the bowl; any farther and we would have flipped. The bow of the raft rose suddenly over the huge back ridge. I dug in with my paddle but found only air. And then we slammed down and a huge wave poured over us—absolutely drenched us. I felt the river's weight, its incredible tonnage, beneath me and all around me. But we had made it through.

The second raft followed and it looked like trouble. Chris Two had brought her raft to the edge of the moon crater but it was sliding down much too far. The raft lost momentum and began a sickening sideways turn. One side shot up and appeared certain to flip. The two paddlers in the bow were catapulted out and disappeared beneath the churning foam. Chris managed to keep her raft upright and dropped her oars to pull one of the men, Montana writer George Wuerthner, from the roaring chute. The other man, David Behar, of San Francisco's Bay Institute, took a longer ride down and drifted toward us through the washout. We backpaddled furiously to intercept him. Joe Daly and I grabbed his flotation vest and together we heaved him gasping into our raft.

• • •

A little later in the summer the Clavey River had dropped a bit but was still fairly high. I'd brought a fly rod and was hiking alone along a bankside path at the bottom of a pitched slope, eyes peeled for poison oak and rattlesnakes. In shorts and low-cut sneakers, I was more than ready for snake country.

This is a tough place to get into, which should be its principal attraction, but could prove its Achilles' heel. Because of its technical difficulty, the Clavey will never be rafted commercially. There are no campsites along the river. And although at times fly fishermen in California seem more numerous than locusts, they have not descended here in their pestilential hordes. This means that it's hard to make an economic argument for saving the Clavey. It might seem heretical even to have to put a price tag on this kind of beauty, but such are the vicissitudes of life in the late twentieth-century.

There is a famous book, a collaboration by the great conservationist David Brower and the wilderness photographer Eliot Porter, called *The Place That No One Knew.* It is an account of how Glen Canyon in Utah was drowned by a massive hydro project because only a handful of people were even aware of the existence of that remarkable declivity in the Utah desert. Stumbling along the rocks, looking down at the dazzling play and sparkle of the water, I thought about nearby Yosemite National Park, how its campgrounds would be filled to capacity on this bright summer weekend. A funny thing about Yosemite, they say it is being loved to death. The opposite is true here. This is the canyon no one knows and the developers are hoping it stays that way. Could white-water rafters and fly fishermen save this river by popularizing it? Of course, the trick will be getting fly fishermen to climb down into this sun-blasted corridor to fish for average-size trout when they could more easily be dragging hogs onto the banks of the East Walker River. Or crossing lines with fifty other anglers on the riffle section below the Hat Creek powerhouse. Or getting mugged outside the Nite Cap Bar in San Francisco's Tenderloin on a Saturday night. California has so much to offer every taste.

I slipped on the bank, barking my shin. It was easily ninety degrees. At least the interface between air and the river would be cool. I waded out into a small pool and pulled a few yards of line off my reel. I figured I'd have about twenty-five yards of fishing room before I'd have to get out and scramble over rocks again. I looked up at the steep walls of the canyon, really a deep and very narrow mountain valley where the river has cut a series of v-shaped troughs through the dun-colored rock. I noticed that closer by the river, the leaves on bankside alders and the tangles of poison oak were a translucent, acid green. The water was extraordinarily clear, too, although I knew better than to drink from it.

A few cattle ranged in the upper reaches. Overhead, a solitary crow yawped at me from the cliff face.

My line tapped twice with an insistence that could only mean a trout. I reeled in a six-inch rainbow. Certainly nothing to get excited about. Except perhaps that lateral flush of rose and lavender that seemed to dissolve into its own translucence. A breeze passed like thin, clear music across the pine-covered slopes.

I fished through the pool and had to admit that on this day the fishing was poor. Time passed slowly, as time should in a canyon. The brightness of noon burned a hole in the sky. There didn't seem to be a single cloud. I dipped my hand into the stream and poured the icy water over my forehead. The sun block I wore started to run and burn my eyes.

I waded out of the pool and made my way along the bank, occasionally tripping over a loose rock or the odd misplaced stone. I thought about hiking well downstream from the Cottonwood Creek Bridge crossing where I had come in. I wanted to see the unusual rock basin that they call God's Bath, where the river crashes through a narrow fissure of nude and polished granite and waterfalls pour into green-blue depths. A large rock outcropping blocked my path to the next pool. I checked carefully for rattlers before reaching for the first hand grip, although it was much too hot for any snakes to be out sunning themselves on the rocks.

My line uncoiled in the air and the fly sank into the rushing throat of the pool. I worked the fly carefully through the length of the crystal run, through each seam in the transparent water.

Moving downstream to the next pool, I worked my fly right up to the lip of a small waterfall. I cast behind rocks and the shadows of rocks. I cast directly into the sunlight that reflected painfully off the water. In the shining turbulence of the flow a rainbow grabbed my fly and broke the surface in a brief but showy display. I'll be generous and say it was nine inches. I know there are big fish in this river, I have seen photographs of them, but they are found mostly down near the mouth. The dam will block the run of big Tuolumne River rainbows that rush up the Clavey to spawn each spring. Don

Moyer, a fly fisherman who lives down in the valley and who haunts these Sierra streams like a wraith, had promised to take me into some of his hot spots, I wished I had taken him up on it. It was clear I had little idea what to do in this high runoff. So late in the season, with the river low, fly fishermen hiked upstream and hooked sackfuls of fish, but they were all pretty small. Mine too.

I figured it had probably taken my nine-incher four years to reach even this size. There was not a lot in the way of insect life in this swift stream. It was easy to understand the lack of company.

Reaching down, I cupped my hand in the river and again poured water over my head. I gazed downstream, studying the canyon from rim to cleft. Heat radiated from the walls, the albedo reflections bending and waving. The only sound was the river rushing.

I proceeded downstream. The Clavey was wadeable but the banks were difficult to walk, particularly where the canyon tended to narrow and pucker. Away from the water, the air once again grew heavy and dense. I started to scale one of the lower slopes that loomed in my way. The scree gave way under my fingers. I clawed my way up and examined the rod for scratches. There were plenty of them. My bare right knee was skinned, too. Sweat dripped into my eyes and once again I felt the sting of melting sun blocking ointment. Somewhere in the canyon, as if to exaggerate the stillness, came the flute-like song of a bird, a half-dozen clear quavers, cool and sweet as a mountain rill.

With stinging eyes, I followed the meander of the river downstream. It looked exactly the same as the water I had been fishing upriver: Parts of the channel here seemed too deep and fast for the fly. The trout were probably holding well below amid the rubble of the bottom.

Why even bother coming down here in the blaze of midday? I asked myself. For that matter, why come to this canyon at all? The meadows along Yellow Creek were more inviting. The Owens had bigger fish and more of them. Fall River was certainly prettier. All were more easily reached. I gazed up at the steep pitch of the slope and then back down into a pool of underwater light: a trout, in the lee of a rock.

I scrambled down the bank and approached the lie from below. I had to be careful. The sun was now over my right shoulder and the shadow of a moving rod and line could easily spook the fish. In three successive casts, I floated a small dry fly over the rock, imagining the trout soaring up for the strike. In fact, the trout gave no sign that it even saw the offering. I walked along the bank upstream and tried to dead-drift a nymph down into the pool. The current swept the fly away, well ahead of the fish. I inched closer, drifting the sunken offering. But a sudden movement of my rod put all the careful stalking to an end. The trout, formerly oblivious, clearly didn't like it and sped off into the dancing molecules of a white-water chute.

I wiped the sweat from my eyes and gazed back at the way I had come. The sky above the canyon seemed white-hot, radiant with light and space. For the hundredth time that day, I noticed there was no one else in the canyon. I was three hours from San Francisco Bay and entirely alone amidst the muted slopes, the seral forest and the white rush of the Clavey River. Beyond the canyon lay even more subcanyons, more sun-blasted mountains and the familiar forests of pine. Nothing much out here at all, come to think of it. Nothing but the vast and silent world.

Stealing Away

In San Francisco the illusion of summer still persists. Cold water wells up from the Pacific, cools the air and condenses into pillows of fog that float under the deck of the Golden Gate Bridge. Foghorns lower and blast for days. On the big coastal rivers, there is a suspicion of stirring and great movement.

All this is confirmed when a friend calls to suggest a fishing trip. He tells you: "I'm in a steelhead frame of mind."

Fishing in a desert, like this one in Oregon, is an ironic act and has a mystical and spooky quality I love. That a cold trout river can run through such a dry and eerie vastness, shimmering with heat, seems less anomaly than miracle. You expect to encounter bleached steer skulls, not trout. But the steelhead of the Columbia drainage have been in the hot Deschutes canyon since July.

Now in late September, wading the edges of the cool, broad river, casting into the sweeping main force of current, we wait for oversize fish to soar up and devour our flies. Although the days are warm, the heat waves and hanging virgas of summer have vanished. Desert nights are cold and sharp, the bankside alders edged in burnt sienna. I count five separate bands of black basalt in the canyon rock above, each an ancient riverbed. Our big dries skate across the broad slicks and suddenly one disappears in a spiral of water, a genuine shock.

A steelhead surges downstream. My companion trips—he looks as if he is genuflecting in the river—his rod bending and recovering furiously. His cheap reel makes more noise than a bad opera. Stumbling out of the water, he gives chase along a pitched bank of very uneven cobblestones and the occasional misplaced boulder. In waders, he is as graceful as Fatty Arbuckle.

The fish darts, turns and holds against the current. My friend cranks his reel madly, only to lose line each time the steelhead punches a new hole in the river. Fifteen minutes later, however, it swims in ever smaller circles, resigned. Led to the beach, the steelhead flops heavily, its powerful, square tail slapping the stones. It is a seven-pound buck, mouth agape, an October caddis buried in the hinge of its jaw. The dorsal fin is stubby, worn smooth; a hatchery fish and a keeper. We have a brief debate over whether to let it go, then make our decision.

Its steaks are broiled over coals in camp at evening as magpies flutter in and out of the sage and the canyon fades away into blackness until all that remains is the sound of the river.

• • •

We have decided to rename all the famous pools on the North Umpqua. The fishing has been that slow. A friend is taken with my observation that the pools in the Camp Water at Steamboat are like good Hollywood character actors. Each is a type, each has its own signature mannerisms. So Kitchen becomes the Warren Oates pool, and the three Mott pools we rename for M. Emmet Walsh. I get to call my favorite pool, Surveyor, after Harry Dean Stanton. We're looking to name a pool for Walter Brennan, but we can't find one that reminds us of a cackling nineteenth-century mule skinner. Our foolishness is interrupted when a steelhead rolls and shatters the green stillness of Boat Pool.

If we stare into the river long enough, we can see steelhead behind boulders and alongside underwater ledges, their graceful bodies tapering down to broad, powerful tails. In lower Kitchen, two fly casters dead-drift heavily weighted nymphs under fluorescent strike indicators. They wear the latest livery from some tony fly shop. As usual, my friend is dressed like a farmer. A purist, however, he asks me if sinking a weighted nymph under an indicator that acts as a drop-hinge can truly be called fly fishing. I tell him this particular controversy means as little to me as sixteenth-century arguments over transubstantiation of the Eucharist.

I move upriver to Surveyor Pool. Surveyor reflects a thick stand of ancient Douglas fir and is the first pool on the Camp Water to catch the afternoon shade. At this hour, the huge shadow on the water renders the pool dark and exquisitely detailed like a Dutch masterpiece. Locating steelhead in a river like the Umpqua is easy; getting them to take the fly is the trick. I have a friend who is something of a horse racing degenerate who loves nothing more than to play the ponies at Golden Gate Fields. He has devised any number of fine systems to handicap them. Like any good fly fisherman, he tends to play the percentages rather than go for the long shots. And so I look for steelhead pretty much where they are expected to be: in deep even riffles and in the body and tailouts of pools like Surveyor. I stare transfixed at the dense, intricate shadow on the water and tell myself, I'll bet this pool holds racehorses.

In northern California most steelhead fishing takes place in winter, so naturally I get in all the dry fly fishing I can. When I see a large orange sedge riding the current depositing an egg sac, no one has to draw me a diagram. The fifth time I send the October caddis skating across the surface of the pool, a steelhead erupts and takes it down in a boil. I am so surprised that at first I fail to strike, which is actually the proper thing to do in this kind of situation. I raise the rod and feel this incredible, living weight. I never quite believe it when it happens; never quite believe a four-ounce fly rod can perform this fabulous conjurer's trick.

The steelhead pulls me all over the pool, ripping out line and sending the water spraying up in thousands of exploding drops.

When I finally get it to the beach, I see that it is a nine-pound hen fish, its flanks an iridescent wash of silver and rose. I revive the steelhead and send it back into the pool. A huge, childish pleasure suffuses me. Hiking back up the Mott Trail, I notice that the dense forest seems to tamp the sound of the river and the sunshine between the fir trees is filled with dancing motes. This giddiness will not leave me.

• • •

I am the only person in the old Orleans Hotel. Even the staff have left for the night. They have handed me the front-door key and given me the run of the place. There's nothing in here worth stealing, anyway. The hotel, a hundred years old, serves as a ramshackle lodge, but tonight it has the unmistakable feel of a haunted house. The only book I have brought along to read is a scary thriller. Appropriate choice. No heat in the place; the deserted Klamath River canyon is freezing in the first big chill.

Earlier that morning, I had hiked down the Goat Trail to Ice Cream Riffle above the highway bridge. The canyon was wreathed in fog and a cold mist obscured the mountains. I could see neither Chimney Rock nor the peak of Medicine Mountain.

I fished small Brindle Bugs and Mossbacks under the riffles until the sun burned through the haze and vapors. Later I worked the long riffle above the huge pool at Dolan's Bar, Wallace Riffle up-river and big Ti-Bar Flat, catching steelhead that locals call "half pounders." I even considered driving all the way up to Tom Martin Creek, for purely literary reasons. It figures in a scene in Richard Brautigan's *Trout Fishing in America*. ("You had to be a plumber to fish that creek.")

The Klamath River holds swollen runs of half pounders. These are adolescent fish that migrated to the sea for only a few months. Many are sexually immature and won't spawn that year. There are two ways to look at this: either you are fishing for the world's smallest steelhead, or California's largest trout. Take your pick.

I go at it all day with my six-weight rod before deciding that trout fishing isn't really what I'm after. I want something epic. I figure if I have any chance of taking a "true" steelhead from the Klamath drainage, say one of about seven pounds or greater, I will have to hike up into its tributary, the Salmon River. Or perhaps fish the pool where the Salmon empties into the Klamath, where big spawners wait to ascend. Some say that the south fork of the Salmon is so cold, its remote pools so crystalline, it holds steelhead even in summer.

And so it's decided. Tomorrow I'll fish the canyon section of the Salmon where it cuts through an almost impenetrable gorge. I'll break out the heavy ordnance: big rod, shooting heads, sinking lines.

All night the Orleans Hotel creaks in the dark like the rigging of an old sailing ship. I dream I am rounding the Golden Gate.

A low December sun backlights bare willows and the water has taken on exaggerated definition. Half the pool lies in deep shadow, half in the light. The pool is known as Bud Hole and flows behind the Foppiano Vineyard on the Russian River south of Healdsburg. The late Raymond Burr's ranch on Dry Creek is around here somewhere.

The Russian's glory is largely squandered, but every once in a while a steelhead like the one hiding in this pool gives you a reason to believe.

There was a time when steelhead poured up the river in Old Testament numbers. Example: in 1942 a quarter of a million fish—steelhead and silver salmon—ran upstream to spawn. These days, anglers are lucky if they see a few hundred steelhead pass through the mouth at Jenner. The problems are various: development in the valley, dams, gravel mining on the upper river, irresponsible forestry, raw sewage. And then there is the uncontrolled growth of irrigated vineyards, each new estate drawing water from precious spawning tributaries. Every time you uncork a bottle of wine marked Sonoma County, the ghost of a steelhead swims out of it.

My fly line soars over the river, highlighted by the setting sun. For once, I have Bud Hole to myself. The steelhead rolls and disturbs the opulent darkness over the pool. I shoot a tight loop to the far bank. Good turnover, maximum distance. I'm a fine caster as long as there are no eyewitnesses to say otherwise. I mend my line to slow the fly's drift as it passes deep through the fish's lie. With just enough tension, it drifts even slower than the current. I do everything by the book, changing flies repeatedly. Nothing happens.

After a half hour of this, an angler with a spinning rod, all nonchalance, ambles down to the dirt bank and sets himself up uncomfortably close to me. He hurls a lure the size of a flashlight into the pool and hooks the steelhead on his second retrieve. The fish leaps twice, sounds and is rudely yanked to the shore. It is seven pounds, bright as chrome. The angler picks it up by the gills and walks away without a word, leaving me dumbfounded, suspended in disbelief. I call it a day.

We decide to fish the Gualala River on Christmas morning. My friend is right. While everyone is worshipping "a vaporous hominoid in the sky," as someone described it, we have Miner Hole to ourselves. Hell, we have the whole damn river. Our damp lines leave trails in the air that fade into misty coronas.

Can steelhead fishing be a valid religious experience? And can you use it to get out of jury duty? We ponder these weighty themes as our flies drift through the tailout.

I hike up the long gravel bar and ford the river below Thompson Hole. It rained along the coast last night, freshening the river. In the morning light, the canyon looks like the pages of an illuminated manuscript. The mossy cliffs are wet and glistening, the redwoods dank and mysterious. The placid river pools are a soft, chalky green, perfect for fly fishing. At the lower end of the pool, I see the faint surface swirl that marks a drowned redwood stump. More of a wrinkle, really. I ease a few casts above it and let my small, dark fly swing past. I work it slowly through the tailout. Steelhead smolts keep bumping against the fly, trying to get their little mouths around the hook. A few succeed. On the big rod they are like weak taps of Morse Code.

I savor the solitary pleasures of the pool, fishing through it twice. When I return to Miner Hole, I see that my friend has a steelhead on in the tailout. Even at this distance I can see it is a tremendous fish. It flashes upstream and jumps, landing with a huge, head-shaking splash. My friend can barely contain its runs. He leans back on his heels and points the butt of the rod at the fish, a huge curve bends into it. This makes for a momentary stalemate. And then suddenly the steelhead rips cross-stream, charging directly at his nemesis. The line goes limp. My friend reels frantically, taking up slack, and the fish jumps again, its silver flank flashing in the morning sunlight, spray flying everywhere. Without warning, it again reverses direction and shoots for the far bank, sending line screaming off the reel.

The fight lasts twenty minutes. When my friend finally manages to ease the creature to shore, we can see that it will probably go about fifteen pounds, a truly awesome fish. My friend grasps it directly above the thick tail. Cradling it with his other hand, he eases the steelhead headfirst into the current, slowly moving it back and forth to let the cold, oxygen-rich water flow through the gills. Revived, the steelhead darts for safety.

A fish like this calls for a round of drinks. But the saloon in the Gualala Hotel is closed because it's Christmas. And we are late getting back to San Francisco too, which poses a problem for my friend. His girlfriend showers him with furious abuse. There is no impromptu awards banquet.

The two men in the dimly lit bar in Garberville are discussing a drug deal. Here in California's Redwood Empire, marijuana is a bigger cash crop than timber. The pair arranges a buy of the fine sensimilla that grows all over the nearby hills and hollows. Things could be worse. I could be in a barroom full of drunken loggers just laid off from the mill. The forests of Humboldt County are filled with crucified spotted owls.

For days, I have been fishing the heart out of the Eel River Canyon. The south fork Eel is low and clear—too low to fish near the town of Leggett. So I focus downriver on a series of emerald pools between Benbow and Garberville and wind up my evenings on Hart's Pool just below the town of Redway. I lose one good steelhead under the monarchs of Alexander Grove off the Avenue of the Giants.

My favorite pool is an enormous pit of green water called Sylvan. One evening, I try to cover the rollers that suddenly appear at the lower end of this but all my casts are futile. I consider trying the remote middle fork, but an angler fishing wee warts and hot shots from the bank tells me that it's still muddied up from a storm that fell over the Yolla Bolly Wilderness a week ago.

Back in town, the big rumor making the rounds is that the brilliant and notoriously reclusive author, Thomas Pynchon, has been hiding out under an assumed identity in Garberville, writing on his novel. There are sightings of this phantom everywhere.

The next day, in a rugged canyon pool below Piercy, I hook and land a bright five-pound hen fish. I take her at high noon, against all the odds. As I release the fish, I hear a disturbance in the air over the canyon. It is the familiar thwock-thwock of an approaching helicopter. I squint into the sun and make out the markings of a DEA surveillance aircraft. Perhaps they are looking for Mr. Pynchon.

Rain falls steadily on San Francisco. I badly need to get out of town. My favorite bars are beginning to resemble steelhead pools.

The Mattole River is out of the question. It sits in a great, dripping rain catch on the Lost Coast. It is possibly the most remote and underrated steelhead river in California, but it's unfishable now.

I drive north for six hours over the rain-slick Pacific Coast Highway and turn right just before

Oregon. Although it is raining softly, the Smith River unrolls like a bolt of green silk through its ancient redwood canyon. The mist rises off the trees like smoke.

I walk up the Hiouchi Trail, padding softly over the forest duff. Towering redwoods stand in otherworldly silence. The light in the canyon is dim and seems to come mostly from the river. The clarity of the pools is startling.

I make out the dark shape of a steelhead finning in the tailout of Bluff Hole. All this cold transparency is deceptive. An illusion. The river is deeper than it looks and I almost ship water into my waders. I quarter my cast downstream and drift the fly toward the steelhead, but it swims off, weightless, on a surge of energy. I reel in and change leaders, selecting one that is the same foliage hue as the river, and I scale down to eight-pound test line. I tie on a small black-and-green fly and carefully fish as much of the lower pool as my casts can reach.

Later, I cross the Hiouchi Bridge so I can fish the other side of Bluff and Park Hole. I start by working the broad, deep riffle above Jedediah Smith Park, making sure to fish the edge of the sweeping current. When I come to the first refulgent pool, I lengthen my leader to fifteen feet. Five drift boats silently pass by in the rain. I am the only fisherman on shore.

The sides of the canyon are exquisite. Dripping thickets of fern rise up from the forest floor. The wet moss on the cliff face is catching the final, dull light of late afternoon and the redwood forest is filled with a dark and earthly splendor.

The iron sky grows heavier, the heavens open. I drag myself out of the river, blinded by the downpour. The river rises five feet overnight.

When I first moved West, a friend assured me that I could fish for salmon or steelhead every day of the year and theoretically that may be possible. After all, a little-known run of spring Chinooks makes it up the Trinity each May, a rare complement to the fall salmon runs. And unique run of unusually powerful summer steelhead ascends the middle fork Eel each spring. Half pounders, they always seem to be hanging around the Klamath regardless of the time of year. Even on the hottest summer day, a steelhead somewhere seeks the caress of water from a cold, spring-fed seepage in a remote mountain pool. The steelhead highway goes on forever.

Not really. It doesn't work that way. This becomes clear on a day in late March when I go up to the Gualala River to fish the run of smaller bluebacks.

A light rain is falling in the canyon. The redwood sorrel that carpets the forest floor is a vivid shamrock green. Earlier, a few fish rolled in the tailout of Miner Hole. The day is so mild, I wonder if one of these steelhead might actually come up to the surface and take a dry fly. Old timers on the river tell me this has never happened.

Once again, I hike up the gravel bar and cross the shallow river below Thompson Hole and again fish the lower end of the pool. It is filled with descending steelhead smolts. An angler on the river says the last bluebacks swept upriver two weeks ago. Anything you catch now will be spawned out, starved and bound for the Pacific. The smolts in Thompson Hole insistently tap the fly, signaling the end and beginning.

In the evening, I walk back down to Miner Hole. A solitary steelhead lolls in the lower pool. Should I bother this ocean-bound, scarred warrior? The walls of the green canyon blur softly in the misting rain. Steelhead season is over.

An Ordinary Creek

We drove out to Winters, my friend Hal complaining all the way about the dreadfulness of California—how it had become a flea market for scavenging lawyers, criminal stockbrokers, advertising goons and real estate sneaks. Look at the crowds. And look at the rivers. There wasn't a commercial guide or outfitter in the state who could tie a blood knot or change a flat tire.

"Mark my words, they'll be moving Orvis to Mexico next," said Hal, muttering fiercely into his beard. The flatlands roared past us as he held the pickup truck at a safe and perfectly reasonable eighty miles per hour.

What had prompted this diatribe was a week of ominous skies and sheets of cold Pacific rain that had blown out the steelhead rivers. Eager to escape, my friend had agreed to accompany me to Putah Creek for a day of winter trout fishing.

A few miles west of Winters we passed the last irrigated groves of almond and apricot trees, and the valley floor rose up gradually into an oak woodland of dark, dripping hills. Below the road, off to our left, the strange bluish waters of Putah Creek poured like a cheap margarita through a dense riparian thicket of alder and brush willows. We followed the river for five miles, coming into a canyon of hogbacks, ridges and high, violent outcroppings which ended at a towering dam that held back the vast impoundment known as Lake Berryessa. The lake was named after the Berryessa family, recipients of the original Spanish land grant for Rancho Las Putas. I don't know what was on their minds, but the word *puta*, from which both the ranch and creek took their names, is Spanish for whore. Somewhere at the bottom of the lake's immense basin many fathoms down and under thousands of tons of pressure, lay the original creekbed.

Runoff swept over the spillway, falling into the lagoon that formed the first pool below the dam. More of a pond, really, it was fringed with beds of coontail and hornwort. Out of this the creek poured into the granitic dullness of the canyon. Below dark ridge lines and oak-covered hills, streamlets overflowed and rainwater dripped from trees, bushes and thorn mazes. From the main channel noise reverberated: the creek bed of crushed chert and peridotite rock. Human voices seemed to fade in and out of these riffles, as if the creek were conducting an argument with itself.

I stared into the water, hoping to spot the mirror flash of a vamping trout. But these were not clear lensed pools. The river carried a cloud of sediment from the silt trap upstream. I couldn't make out a single rock on the creek bottom; I could only guess at its depth.

"Think of it as flowing like a lush chardonnay," said Hal, doing his best Ernest Schwiebert imitation.

"I understand the creek has a very high pH factor," I said.

"Did you know that human urine has the same pH level as a can of Mountain Dew? I read that in *Newsweek*."

We backtracked down the road until we came upon a dirt corral crowded with four-wheel-drive vehicles. Stoned teenagers played their radios louder than chainsaws, creating an omnipresent endangered-forest mood. Fly fishermen stood beside Chevy Suburbans, struggling into waders or joining graphite rods at the ferrules, ignoring the flash of beer cans and the riffs of Pearl Jam rocking above the evergreens. We slid in next to a battered Ford Ranger with a bumper sticker that read: "We Interrupt This Marriage to Bring You Deer Hunting Season." Once again I marveled at the fact that these days a 7.2-liter V-8 engine is indispensable to modern life. Pickup trucks are keenly popular in San Francisco, where half the residents seemed to be secretly employed as ranch hands and alfalfa farmers.

I glanced over at the creek, Bedlam. One of the Bay Area fly shops had a class under way. Hal announced he would start his own fishing clinic. It would be limited to downtown lawyers and grant foundation executives. They would be instructed to hold live maggots in their mouths to warm the bait. Each session would begin with one hundred pushups.

We suited up. Hal carefully joined the shafts of his bamboo rod. Hiking out of the parking lot, we crossed a wooden footbridge that spanned a gushing feeder creek. In summer it was an empty, stone gulch. During the drier months, dust settles like sifted flour on the hills. In *Assembling California* John

McPhee wrote that the hillsides here become so parched that geologists striking hammers against the rocks accidentally spark brushfires.

The hills today were cloaked in a luxuriant mantle of greenery, the drooping grasses and blue oaks heavy with winter rain. An aroma of dank decay rose sharply off the banks. The canyon was lush and dense and would have seemed completely wild except for the utility lines that stretched over the hills, reaching out toward the towering dam. We scrambled down the steep granite embankment and joined a pair of anglers who were emerging from the creek. Hal introduced me as the steelhead columnist for the *Christian Science Monitor*. We asked what the trout were taking and we were advised that they were taking very small nymphs fished exceedingly deep.

I stepped into the creek, my boots scraping the chert bottom, and immediately I felt the deep draw of water all around me, the sensation of being bound for parts unknown. The current felt both complicated and urgent, its motion built into it by the contours of the land upstream and down. Just standing in a river, any river, makes me feel vital and continuous. The pull of water is so profound that often I am reluctant to leave a stream. There is a kind of joyousness to just standing there, feeling the play of the earth's motion.

I stared deeply into the sediment-filled creek, thinking that nymphing trout might perhaps somehow show themselves like glints of mica in hard granite. But it was impossible to see anything. You had to be an existentialist to fish this creek. I made a cast upstream and mended line to allow my nymph to float deeply on a tensionless leader. I did this many times, slack-lining the tumbling nymph over the creek bottom until the tip of my line at last halted in midfloat. I raised the rod on a living, struggling weight. It seemed as much a shock as a mystery. But the fish came off immediately—I saw its underwater evanescent swirl—and that was that.

As I made another cast to the head of the run, I felt the sky closing in on us. A squall line was moving through. Rain poured down: clear, heavy beads rattling the treetops, pounding the surface of the creek white and gray. A roar went up from the canyon. I endured the steady drumming on my poncho and thought about the thermos of coffee in the pickup. The Zen philosopher Dogen, awakened suddenly at night, called the sound of rain on the temple roof "the one true thing." The *roshis* and *tanka* poets of thirteenth-century Japan understood.

The squall line passed across the hills, broke up and reformed somewhere over the valley. You could feel the barometer rise. The canyon reappeared once more as dense, wet thicket and dripping embankment, the creek magically restored as fly water.

The air over Putah Creek felt energized. Everyone on the water was hyper. With each cast came the knowledge that one might suddenly pull up on the kind of dream trout normally confined to trophy rivers in Montana. The presence of six- and seven-pound rainbows and even a few browns in the creek went a long way toward explaining the popularity of what was otherwise a silt-laden irrigation ditch bound for the central valley.

I fished through the run slowly, working my way downstream, the bottom gradually falling out from under me. Beyond lay an unwadeable green trench through which the current passed like a cold shock. Here the creek bulged against a granite bank that rose sharply on the outside curve, full of alder branches, tangled roots and overhanging trees. Undoubtedly trout would be holding in the deep water along the edge. But there was no way I could reach them.

I climbed out of the creek and took a hike downstream. The public lot was still full although the sallow teenagers had departed, perhaps on another beer run. I found the path leading down to where the creek passes under the highway bridge and I followed the trail through a maze of thorn bushes that grew well above my head, coming out at last onto a muddy bank just upstream of the bridge, its understory a great span of attic gloom that rumbled mightily under each passing car. I waded ankle-deep over streaming cobblestones to get below the highway span. Here lay a run of interesting pocket water that narrowed into a swift chute as the creek tried to squeeze by a clump of brushy islands. There was a campsite for trailers located directly upstream and the breeze blowing along the creek carried with it the unmistakable fetor of open septic tanks. You weren't going to see this place anytime soon on the cover of *Esquire Sportsman*.

I waded midstream toward a cluster of boulders, the projecting points of rock barely breaking the surface. Here was a comfortable spot from which I could launch my casts and get good, long drifts from my nymph. It was perhaps too obvious a choice, easy water pounded hard by other fishermen. But I managed to take two modest trout from these niches. They were stream-bred rainbows, their sides a pinkish rose. I had attached a fluorescent strike indicator to my leader to detect the subtler takes. My friend was upstream, so there was no chance of his seeing this apostasy; I wouldn't want to offend fly fishing's sternest Calvinist.

I rejoined him. He said he wanted to fish the "frog water," the pond below the dam. So I borrowed the keys to his pickup and drove downriver, searching for official streamside access points maintained by a stolid county parks commission. I pulled into the first one and found out that I would have to stuff a couple bucks into an envelope just for the privilege of parking the truck. This so-called "day use" fee apparently went toward defraying the park commission's costs of maintaining the stream, which as far as I could tell seemed to consist solely of sending someone around at the end of each day to collect the money. For more than a dozen years, bankside litter removal and stream-restoration projects have been carried out by volunteers calling themselves the Fly Fishers of Davis.

The thicket alongside the creek was dense enough to get turned around in. I followed the pathway deep into the labyrinth and came at last upon the riverbank hemmed with overhanging alders. The air was redolent of the earthen fragrance of logjams. The spot was close and grotto-like. Again I seemed to hear voices in the running water. I followed the path downstream a good ways until I came upon a clearing of downed limbs and bunched meadow grass. The creek was very deep here and appeared to have had much of its mysterious inner life channeled away. Still, I could wade out a few feet before the bank slipped away entirely, and I had just enough room for a backcast.

Like the creek upstream, the water here was dully opaque. I dropped the nymph into pockets between river rocks, which appeared as vague, ghostly blurs beneath the green running channel. The nymph disappeared into invisible lies and I imagined it drifting just millimeters above the moss and stones. It was like fishing in a shroud. My mind wandered badly and I found myself imagining Pacific harvest trout in tidal lagoons and salmon in redwood streams; here and there a few migratory steelhead appeared within an Idaho desertscape and cutthroats swam prominently in Wyoming rivers.

My line point halted in midfloat and I had just enough presence of mind to raise the rod on an exploding trout. There was a series of quick, jabbing bursts and then a long, focused dash upstream. The reel made a few customary shrieks and the hookup felt staunch. The trout tore off on a final, dogged run. Eventually I was able to ease it toward the bank. I got below the fish and let the current glide the trout over onto my sunken palm, where it hovered in perfect equipoise. I raised my hand to lift the fish, the water streaming off its bright back. It was a German brown, all silver and wintry under a deep mantle of black spots.

I returned the fish to the stream and marched out of the creek. As I reached the truck, a few heavy raindrops spattered the roof and windshield. I climbed into the cab and watched the rain bead on the glass. Fiddling with the AM band, I managed only to tune in a succession of radio talk shows; there didn't seem to be a civil tongue in all of California. And then suddenly there was Neil Young coming out of the speakers, a splendid surprise. His eerie, underwater voice filled the cab with sweet, breathless song. I gazed out the windshield into the plainness of the day, squinting hard through the glittering rain. It was, after all, only an ordinary creek, but for the moment there was radiance and rapture all around.

Home Waters

The coast was gray-lit by fog. I was driving out to Bolinas to visit an acquaintance, Josiah Thompson, an ex-college professor who had become a rather renowned private detective. Tink, as he is known, had given up a tenured position at Haverford College in Pennsylvania to become a private eye.

As usual, the little coastal village of Bolinas was swallowed in summer fog. Driving over the Bolinas Ridge, past the Audubon Canyon Ranch, I kept alert for the unmarked turnoff; the state of California keeps putting up CalTrans signs to mark the way, which the residents, who hate visitors, keep tearing down. Bolinas is a last vestige of the sixties, an artist and hippie colony where the scent of hash and patchouli oil still mixes with the sea air.

When the fog lifts, Bolinas is faintly visible from my apartment in San Francisco. Although San Francisco is a city in every sense of the word, everywhere I look, the Pacific wilderness is barely at bay. Never have I seen an urban landscape where the outline of the natural world is still so manifest, so dramatic, where the memory of how it was remains so insistent.

When I reached the turnoff, striped bass were feeding at the mouth of the lagoon and the fog lay like a cottony white whale over Duxbury Reef. I drove past the old house where the poet Richard Brautigan had committed suicide a decade ago and found my way to Horseshoe Lane and my friend's cabin overlooking the lagoon.

Over drinks, Tink casually mentioned that his son, while fooling around on a little feeder creek one winter, had snuck up on a five-pound steelhead and had plucked it out of the water with his bare hands.

I cherish that image. It reminded me of a secluded canyon sunk into the Marin Headlands. In it is the ancient redwood forest known as Muir Woods. I like it best in late autumn-early winter when the rainy season begins. The air is sharp with the scent of bay laurel growing near the creek. The tourists have gone and, as the days pass, the soft patter of rain grows to a relentless drumming on the redwood canopy. In the first truly heavy downpour, Redwood Creek swells and bursts the sandbar at its outlet at Muir Beach. Salmon rush upstream to spawn, followed later by steelhead.

Although the stream is protected and cannot be fished, I like to walk the creek trails looking for rose flashes in the water. The salmon distribute themselves well upstream. A few make it beyond the fourth footbridge; a few move up Fern Creek. In the dank splendor after a rainfall, mushrooms bloom on the forest floor. Some, like the slender mycena and the yellow witch's butter, seem to glow with the brilliance of undersea coral.

Driving up one winter's day to Point Reyes where there is whale watching, I was hoping to spot gray whales passing offshore on their annual migration to Baja. It was a cold, bright day, clear enough to see all the way to the Farallon Islands. Driving over the Marin Headlands, you pass peaceful farms, windswept beaches and lightly traveled country roads. Not far from the little town of Inverness, I stopped at the Highway 1 bridge overlooking Lagunitas Creek, which used to be called Paper Mill. The creek drains the rugged western slope of Mount Tamalpais and pours into the head of Tomales Bay. I gazed at the glittering tidal flats and in the distance watched a bank of wheeling gulls turning in the air like a child's mobile. I suspected that steelhead were moving upstream in the creek. Earlier in the season, a vestigial run of silver salmon had made it up to Lagunitas to spawn. At one time the salmon fishing in the tidal pools was legendary. But that was before the creek was dammed in order to create the county's reservoir system and fill the hot tubs of Marin. Lagunitas is closed to all fishing now in order to protect what remains of the anadromous runs. Because I had a fly rod stashed in the trunk of my car, I considered driving a little farther up Highway 1 to Walker Creek, at the mouth of Tomales Bay. There was a rumor going about that a Santa Rosa man had caught and released a twenty-pound steelhead there earlier in the week. Torn, I chose Point Reyes and the whales. Perhaps resisting the urge would build character.

The first time I ever fished for Pacific salmon, it was in a river only seventy-five miles north of my apartment. The fact that I didn't have to fly to Alaska to do this had left me feeling just a little smug. True, the Russian River in Sonoma County wasn't the Alagnak, nor was it exactly brimming with fish.

But that autumn a decent run of silvers had entered the lower river along with a few good king salmon. They were said to be stacking up in a pair of pools directly below the Austin Riffle.

I took River Road to get there, rolling past vineyards and fruit stands loaded with pumpkins so bright as to be almost surreal. I sped in and out of redwood groves, through pockets of light and shadow, ignoring hand-lettered signs announcing cider and rental canoes and housekeeping cabins, hardly bothering to slow down for small river towns like Forestville, Rio Nido and Duncans Mills. The river that day was low and extremely clear, the water unusually transparent. Brown's Pool was a stony, illuminated basin of shimmering jade.

I moved downstream to the pool known as Watson's Log. A salmon revealed itself with a loud surface slap. Another fly fisherman covered the salmon with a long, beautiful throw; there was a kind of grandeur to the cast. The fish hit his fly; the rod yielded and then strained impossibly, pulled toward the far bank. It was a king salmon, an athenaeum of primordial knowledge. Using an inner compass, sensing subtle changes in season and the day's length, this salmon had traveled through an open ocean, somehow always fixed on bearings that would lead it to its home stream. Defying astronomical odds, it had navigated back to the river of its birth to spawn and die—one of the most stirring and dramatic spectacles—only to run afoul at Watson's Log on a sparsely tied number-eight orange Comet. But the angler pried the fly from the cartilaginous operculum where it had lodged, and released the fish.

As I stood in the pool, feeling the many threads of the river gather and pull me, I gazed about and thought that the Russian River below Austin Creek seemed a remnant of what the entire valley must have looked like at one time: forests of redwood and Douglas fir up the steep banks. Sheep and dairy cattle grazing peacefully on the distant green hilltops. Osprey soaring high above Austin Riffle, then making a sudden, heart-stopping plunge to the water. I followed its flight until losing it somewhere in between the sun and sky.

But it's not all like this. If a salmon is a brilliant repository of stored genetic knowledge, then what has happened on the Russian River is the equivalent of the sacking of the Library at Alexandria. The salmon now come out of hatcheries. Only a vestige of the wild steelhead run remains, fallen victim to suburban growth that has spread along the valley like an underwater algal bloom.

I heard that steelhead were suspended in the Johnson Beach pool in the funky little river town of Guerneville, which seemed to have as many gay bars as the Tenderloin. I had never fished Johnson's pool and was looking forward to seeing it. When I arrived, a few winos on the beach were enjoying something refreshing out of a brown paper sack. Three young stragglers were engaged in an earnest discussion concerning a lost unemployment check, a DUI conviction and the likely location of a missing firing pin on a .38 caliber walnut-grip Smith & Wesson revolver.

I joined two other fly fishermen on the bank. If the beach at our backs resembled a municipal slum, at least the view downriver, with the banks enveloped in trees, opened out upon a grand democracy of waters. One of my companions landed a large fish and maneuvered it over to the beach with considerable authority. It looked like it would go seven pounds. About that time, a young man ambled over to admire the steelhead. He suddenly expressed his desire to move to the river.

"Do you know if there's a drug problem here?" he asked, somewhat abruptly. He had shoulder-length hair and, for all I knew, he could have been a Seattle grunge musician or an out-of-work tree surgeon.

"When I was his age," muttered the man who had caught the fish, "the only drug problem we talked about was how much the stuff cost."

One mile downstream was Bohemian Grove. The chill air over the valley was pungent with woodsmoke and I found myself fishing a stretch of the river called Hatchers. The run lies just below a summer crossing bridge that is removed at season's end to allow for the migration of salmon and steelhead. I gazed downstream to where the river began its curve into an impressive, deeply forested oxbow. It would eventually pass by Bohemian Grove. This tract was owned by San Francisco's exclusive Bohemian Club which each summer hosted a festive encampment of the nation's richest and most powerful business and political leaders. For a week the honored guests, including statesmen and even a few ex-presidents, stood around complimenting each other on their deep insights and overall venality, and in the general goonery they are said to revert to uninhibited natural states. Picture your least favorite statesman standing naked under a redwood tree with a cocktail glass in hand and you get the idea. Personally, I'll take the winos on Johnson Beach.

Reconciled to the fact that I will never be invited to Bohemian Grove, I made for Monte Rio, a picturesque junkyard village directly downstream. Monte Rio perhaps can best be described as a kind of hybrid hippie-welfare hamlet and river resort, a place where—as its poetic citizens like to put it— "the sleaze meets the trees," a town so small drivers don't bother to signal because "everybody knows where everybody's going anyway." I remembered a day in mid-January when I had been assured I could pull a steelhead out of the Monte Rio Riffle if only I was willing to put up with the dismal view of the municipal beach parking lot and the old Rio movie theater. It was clear when I got there that this was a place where the Pacific wilderness had been held mostly in check. Remembering how depressed I was by the scene and the lack of fish the last time, the only thing I could bear to do was continue down the Bohemian Highway to the little town of Occidental. There I ate a huge Italian feast in a century-old edifice called the Union Hotel. People have been driving to Occidental to do this for ages. That evening, a Friday, roughly five hundred diners passed through the hotel to mop up gargantuan platters of antipasto, ravioli and chicken.

One of the pleasures of fishing rivers so near San Francisco is that much of the harmless eccentricity of the city has carried over into the Russian River valley itself. The number of crackpot designs on the land, for example. The Russian River region has been home to three utopian communities.

The first was the vineyard commune of Icaria Speranzia, whose fifty-five members made it a point to speak only in French. These nineteenth-century utopians pooled all their worldly goods and credited each other with labor premiums. This arrangement lasted five years, until the recession of 1886. Next came Altruria, named after a justly obscure William Dean Howells novel. It was founded by Bay Area egalitarians who acquired 185 acres on Mark West Creek on the Santa Rosa plain. Being visionaries, they planned to dam the creek for hydroelectric power and build a huge tourist hotel. This captured the attention of Ambrose Bierce, cynic and columnist for the San Francisco *Examiner*, who wrote: "Of the amiable asses who have founded the Altrurian colony at Mark West it ought to be sufficient to explain that their scheme is based upon the intellectual diversions of such humorists as Plato, More, Fourier, Bellamy and Howells. That assures the ludicrous fizzle of the enterprise." And so it did. In June, 1895, the colony ran out of cash.

But Fountain Grove sprang up in a valley north of Santa Rosa. Founder Thomas Lake Harris, "primate" of the Brotherhood of New Life, preached Christian mysticism, Swedenborgian spiritualism and what was widely misinterpreted by outsiders at the time as "free love." In truth, Harris was a celibate. But a muckraking exposé of his purported immorality prompted abandonment of Fountain Grove.

Much is gone, driven off by man, yet much remains. Ospreys still soar above the rivers. Deer forage in the dim woods and foggy river bottoms. The air is sharp with woodsmoke and the deep balsamic odor of pines. And salmon and steelhead stubbornly return as they have always, to spawn in their home waters.

Cutthroat Country

I was hanging out in Laguna Beach, one of those small resorts strung along the coast of Southern California like a set of false pearls. It was August and I was staying in a little cottage nestled into a marine terrace high above the ocean. My days were given over to beach bumming; my nights to sensory derangement.

It's a given that cutthroats are stupid fish—although considering what one is willing to pay for a graphite rod these days, who are fly fishermen to judge them?

When it comes to cutthroats, I have behaved foolishly myself and would again.

Outside my window, the Pacific glittered and the sea wind carried the scent of wild anise from the bluffs. Coyotes prowled the cliffs above a blaze of coastal chaparral and all day long you could hear the traffic hissing.

The lassitude of the West Coast was weighing me down. It occurred to me I was due for a change of scene. There is the feeling that a fishing trip wipes the slate clean and although this has never proved strictly true for me, a road trip to the Rocky Mountain West suddenly seemed in order. Abruptly I decided that nothing less would do than to fish for wild native cutthroats in pure mountain streams. I packed my bags and by midnight was ready. I told a friend: "I'm in a Wyoming state of mind."

Interstate 5 disappeared under my headlights, as I accelerated in and out of lane changes, floating low on a cushion of torque. The car's irregular weight tilted faintly on the curves, cities dimmed and brightened, stars faded in and out; Santa Ana became Anaheim became Yorba Linda and the illuminated grid of Southern California spread out before me like a navigation map to the end of the night.

Two hours out of Barstow, the sun rose hard over the desert basin. The light was the color of poured orange juice. On each side of the highway, as far across the desert as I could see, the dark arms and stretching shadows of a thousand Joshua trees rose up like a hosanna out of the light and morning heat. I stared into the sun with closed eyelids but could still see the flaring yellow star through my skin.

There's nothing like travel to narrow the mind. Deep into Nevada I was tailgating land yachts, the great rolling aluminum hell of American tourism. Motor homes as big as Anglican cathedrals blocked the highway and I passed them in an aureole of my own blood pressure. Stopping at a gas station to wash my face, and gazing into the mirror, I couldn't help but notice that I was beginning to look like a drifter on a three-state killing spree.

Utah floated by, a dream of iron oxide, green pines and buff sandstone. Canyon country. High red desert. Rouge cliffs rising up against a sky as blue as the Blessed Mother's cloak. At day's end, a deep sunset fell like spun gold onto the billowing clouds and the eastern sky faded into blue blackness.

I checked into a motel in the tiny Mormon desert town of Nephi, just off Interstate 15. It took an hour for the ancient air conditioner to crank up and cool off the room. In the meantime, I went out to celebrate with a huge steak dinner, barbecued potatoes, great slabs of Texas toast and weak Colorado beer. That night I slept like a dead man.

I drove north into Idaho, the desert giving way to mountain meadows, aspens and lodgepole pines. At Targhee Pass, I crossed the Continental Divide and slipped into Montana, the Yellowstone plateau looming before me under thunderclouds. By dusk I had made the little town of West Yellowstone. I couldn't have been happier if I was in Paris.

Summer, that lovely tourist season, was in full swing. West Yellowstone was lit up like a pinball machine on replay. I'd never seen so many motels in one place.

Tourists streamed in and out of the covered mall and kids mobbed the Dairy Queen. Ludicrous stuffed bears leered from shop windows alongside T-shirt displays, Old Faithful ashtrays, plastic tomahawks and Indian war bonnets with dyed feathers. "Navajo" rugs that looked like dishrags were being hawked in open air stalls for twenty bucks apiece, and just about everything in town looked like it came from either Hong Kong or Seoul. It was still light out, so the town's five fly shops were open, their cash registers singing. The first thing I noticed were the rows of wooden boxes holding exquisitely tied flies, tens of thousands of them. More Asian slave labor, probably. I noticed that the price of a float trip had jumped to two hundred dollars.

I took a cheap motel room on the edge of town, had a chicken fried steak at Huck's Cafe and then walked over to the Stage Coach Inn for a beer to rinse away the road dust. The bar was a haze of blue smoke and voices straining to rise above the roar of the jukebox and the clinking of glasses. A trio of guides sat at the bar nursing long necks, discussing a hatch of flying ants on the Henry's Fork, apparently of biblical proportions. For the first time in weeks I felt at home. Tomorrow I planned to indulge in some of the last great fly fishing in North America.

At the west entry to Yellowstone National Park, I paid my entrance fee and picked up the free fishing license. Over the radio in the booth, a calm, official voice was reporting that a visitor's poodle had just parboiled itself to death by jumping into a hot pool at Midway Geyser Basin. The ranger manning the booth tried not to laugh and almost succeeded. I set off into the pine-covered Madison Valley, trailing behind a recreational vehicle big enough to block out the sun, a two-bedroom condo on wheels.

Somewhere near the park entrance I crossed the Montana border into Wyoming. The Madison Plateau, a ridge of black rhyolite, rose up on my right. To my left, the shallow riffle water of the Madison River came into view, guarded by a high sagebrush bank on the far slope. The river deepened and slowed and glided under a bridge, where it passed in fine strands through waving water weeds, springcreek style. Two anglers stood thigh-deep casting slow, easy lines in a graceful aerial ballet that matched the mood of the day. Female elk and their calves grazed sweetly on the marshy banks and tourists poured out of their cars to photograph them. I swung around the R.V., which had suddenly pulled over to the side of the road, its driver—in the grand tradition of all park visitors—not having bothered to signal.

At Madison Junction, where the Gibbon and Firehole Rivers joined in a bench meadow to form the Madison, a solitary buffalo, as big and solemn as a war monument, and as yet unnoticed by the tourists, rested on its haunches in the shade of some lodgepole pines.

I followed the Gibbon east into its canyon and passed a traffic jam at its high falls. Hawks rode the updrafts and ravens lingered by the roadside. An enormous bull elk was trying to graze in peace on the far riverbank. Its massive rack looked polished and wicked, minus the soft velvet of early summer. Tourists abandoned their cars to approach it, Instamatics and camcorders held high.

A mile below this scene, I pulled my car over onto the side of the road and walked down to the river through the lodgepole pines. A hundred feet off the highway, I was completely alone, swallowed in eternal forest-silence. After some minutes, I scrambled back up the hill to the car, eager to get to the trout.

A mile or two further down the road, the forest opened up onto Elk and Gibbon Meadows. At Norris Junction, I turned right and climbed to the forested plateau. By the time I reached the headwaters at Virginia Meadows, the Gibbon was nothing more than a narrow ditch twisting through emerald grass.

At Canyon Junction, I turned north to go up the Washburn Range and the dizzying Dunraven Pass. The park spread out well below me to the east, and I watched wisps of steam rise from geysers and distant fumaroles, floating up from the green forest like the ghosts of Indian campfires. The road, a series of switchbacks, fell through stands of aspen, dropping into dry sage and scattered juniper. At Tower Junction, I turned east, where the Lamar River squeezed into a rough canyon before opening upon a broad, marshy valley. A herd of park buffalo had spread itself out over a meadow shelf well above the riverbank. The air was sharp with the sting of sage.

The Lamar was empty—not a solitary angler on it. No doubt the fly-fishing hordes were in the high meadows of Slough Creek, exercising any number of baseless prejudices in favor of that tributary stream. So much the better. There was a certain gravel shelving bar on this river that I managed to visit in complete privacy each year I came—a pool of pale, greenish water pressed against a grassy, undercut bank. Although Lamar cutthroats have a reputation for moving around in the river, never keeping to one place, I had always found a pod of sixteen-inch cutthroats waiting for me in this minor hole.

I found the cutbank after a short hike, tied on a small gray fly that resembled nothing in particular, and floated it down the throat of the pool. The fly disappeared in a sudden cranberry and olive swirl.

The fish I brought to my hand five minutes later seemed as violently colored as a tropical orchid. Its olive back, mantled in a sparse leopard spotting, melted into sides of yellow butter and apricot that reflected a faint rose and cranberry hue. On its lower jaw, and spreading across its gill plate, was the vivid reddish orange flush that gave the cutthroat its famous name. It was a trout the color of a knife fight.

Out here in the West, cutthroats enjoy a mixed press. "They're stupid fish" is the most common complaint, often uttered by an angler who paid upwards of ninety-five dollars for his vest. Cutthroats are foolish and reckless, goes the complaint, traits I identify with. These critics are fishermen who like to talk about the "challenge" of rainbow trout and speak in reverential tones of the purported "intelligence" of browns, as if fishing for them might be an act worthy of a MacArthur Foundation Grant. But I greatly admired the bold, reckless nature of cutthroats. These cuts in the Lamar ripped my line all over the pool and in a single hour, I took nine trout from this one high bank, one a trophy of eighteen inches.

I drove upriver along the northeast entrance road until coming to Soda Butte Creek, a glittering gravel run that poured into the duller sheen of the Lamar. Here at this confluence, the Lamar turned away from the road, and the river seemed to spring mythically from the dusty, primeval valley. To the south, the bare granite peaks of the Absarokas rose above the treeline, draped in violent thunderclouds. I knew that when the storm hit, the rainwater would cascade off the nude granite and pour down the narrow canyon, turning the pale river the color of coffee ice cream. I took five small cutthroats out of Soda Butte's crystal channel and then started up the trailhead following the Lamar. A turbulent gray light flooded the crooked valley. A lone buffalo rolled in the dust beside the trail and a coyote calmly watched my progress from the edge of the sagebrush. I managed to take several modest cutthroats out of the deeper curves before turning back to escape the storm. I made it back to the car under a rattling fall of hailstones.

• • •

There was a tourist traffic jam on the Grand Loop Road just below the buffalo-grass meadow of Hayden Valley. Bison were trying to cross the roadway and tourists were vaulting from their cars to take pictures, oblivious to the fact that buffalo are responsible for more comic deaths in the park than grizzlies.

The Yellowstone tourist is the world's bravest. He sits his children on the backs of bison to take their photograph. He points his camcorder into the bloodshot eyes of moose and elk. He marches up trails closed by grizzly bear signs and thinks it might be alright to swim in the hydrogen sulfide spring. Later he looks for someone to sue for his injuries, litigation having replaced baseball as the national pastime.

I eased my car around the jam and drove on to the old picnic grounds at Buffalo Ford on the Yellowstone River. The river glided along slowly enough, but with a suggestion of great undertow and power. From the moment I stepped into the river, I felt its numbing coldness and relentless current. The calm glassiness of the water was deceiving. Just standing still, I could feel a steady sliding of gravel under my feet. As I waded out toward midstream, the powerful current seemed to lift me off the clean gravel bottom. I made my slow passage midstream to the lee of a lodgepole-covered island and there carefully positioned myself to be waist-deep in the heart of the greatest concentration of cutthroat trout on the planet. The fish at my feet appeared as red shadows beneath the swirling water.

Trout slowly rose to something tiny in the surface film, feeding steadily, drifting back and forth at leisure, their surface dimples disappearing downriver like smoke rings. I tied on an olive emerger and before long felt the satisfactory tug and pleasing weight of a three-pound cutthroat trout. I took trout after trout off the sandy shelf below the island where the two channels merged. When the hatch of tiny olives ended, I switched over to a small hopper and worked it successfully through the choppy run between the island and the west bank. Later I got bored and just for fun started sliding dry flies steelhead style, creating great waking vees over the surface of the flats. Drag is supposed to scare trout. Instead these produced the most violent, boiling rises of the day. On average, the cutthroats were larger than the ones I had caught on the Lamar, their cranberry and magenta markings deeper and more brilliant.

Sometime around midafternoon, I heard deep grunts and a low, muffled rumbling of the earth coming out of the ponderosa and lodgepole forest on the east bank. I moved away from the island, into the deeper water of the channel just as one of Yellowstone's great bison herds emerged from the forest to ford the river. I counted ninety-six of them making the crossing.

Buffalo are not scary until you see one up close. I mean *really* close. One bitter September afternoon many years earlier, I was fishing a short cascade and plunge pool on the Firehole River above the iron bridge on the old Fountain Freight Road. The low bank at my back was covered in the whitish sinter found around geysers. I was concentrating on a deep aerated hole below a riffle when I suddenly experienced the uncanny sensation that I was being stared at. Expecting to see a park visitor behind me, I turned. Three or four feet away, close enough to reach out and touch, stood a huge bull buffalo patiently waiting to cross the river where I stood. I had no idea how long he had been there.

It stared back at me with black, uncomprehending eyes, a rope of snot hanging from one nostril, a halo of flies swarming about its outsized head. I was close enough to wipe its nose. I hauled ass out of the water, tripping on submerged ledges and lava outcroppings, allowing the great beast to make its dull-witted, lumbering passage across the Firehole.

Yellowstone was like that for me. On another occasion, one August, I was on the trail to Pelican Creek, a step ahead of thunderclouds. Like a good tourist, I had ignored the posted grizzly warnings at the trailhead and had chosen to hike in alone. Now, each time I walked into a pine copse I could enjoy the cheap thrill of knowing there might be something in there that could kill me. As Samuel Johnson might have said, had he been discussing nature instead of public hangings, there's nothing like the prospect of a grizzly bear attack to concentrate the mind wonderfully.

Pelican Creek was a long shot. In early summer it gets a huge spawning run of cutthroats out of Yellowstone Lake. But it was late in the season, and the best I could hope for was a few holdover fish in the upper creek. The trade-off was the spectacular remoteness of it all. The creek wound its way through a huge amphitheater of grass, a subalpine meadow fringed by lodgepole pines and high, crumbling bluffs.

The sky looked discouragingly black. I could practically taste the magnetic resonance in my mouth. From the Mirror Plateau to the north came the low, far-off rumble of thunder and every now and again the horizon would go off like a flashbulb. I could picture massive pines and firs being lashed. I figured one or two hours of fishing before the Apocalypse.

I tied on a hopper and worked it along an undercut bank. The wind kicked up, and I jumped at every rolling pebble, each snapping twig under my boot. The graphite rod in my hand hummed like a transformer. Finally, a cutthroat slashed at my fly and sheared line off the reel. It was a beautiful trout of sixteen inches, as vivid and wild as the impending storm.

 I threw my rod as far as I could and curled up against the embankment. Thunderclouds blotted out the sky. I wrapped my poncho about me and cowered under the onslaught. On a ridge above me, a bush disintegrated in a blue-white flash. Another thunderburst, this one closer, exploded right between my eyes and burned the valley into my brain like an overexposure. I sat out the storm in a frisson of terror.

It is a poor man who frees himself from danger.

Dawn: nature's rush hour. The lodgepole forest concealed a chorus of birds; the world chirped and flourished. I rolled out of my down bag and rubbed the sleep from my eyes. The air was cold, colder than the river water; a wraithlike mist hovered over the Madison.

I put on a sleeveless parka and broke camp as the rest of the park began to stir. My car hit potholes and frost heaves all the way to Norris. Heading north, I passed old Soldier Station, piss yellow Lemonade Lake and dead quiet Roaring Mountain with its barely active fumaroles whose vents barely steamed. A moose chewed on the low willows along Indian Creek, dipping its enormous head under the river. When it rose up, water poured off its massive, palm-shaped antlers. Ravens stood on the roadside, as black as chess pieces.

Beyond the lodgepole forest, I rolled out onto a dry and fragrant sagebrush flat. The road aimed for a cut in the yellow rock and, as I descended, I watched Glen Creek make its rocky drop over narrow Rustic Falls. The car wound through gray travertine hoodoos swept down by ancient landslides. At Mammoth Hot Springs, the waters bubbled up over live terraces like limestone fizz. I slowed to a crawl at park headquarters; a bull elk with a trophy rack of antlers rested on its haunches in front of the superintendent's office.

I made for the park's northern entrance, dipping into the canyon between Mount Everts and Sepulcher, and crossing the Gardner River twice. Somewhere around here I left Wyoming and crossed into Montana, passed through the park entrance booth, the old Roosevelt Arch on my right, and entered the town of Gardiner.

The Yellowstone River flows through it, splitting the town into stunned halves. Beyond the tourist hokum that has grown up around the park, you can see poverty in the tin roofs and imagine barely furnished rooms lit by naked ceiling bulbs. All the bars looked mean and open for business to drunks, ranch hands and elk horn poachers. Outside of town a kid passed me doing eighty; in Montana the legal driving age is fifteen.

I followed the Yellowstone River into Yankee Jim Canyon. Already there were drift boats on the water, the guides working tight to the banks. I imagined myself on the river in the big McKenzie drifts.

Coming out of Yankee Jim Canyon, the valley of the Yellowstone opened before me and the Absarokas rose up on my right like galleons in full sail, the mountains full of blue light and ideas. The river was a ribbon of brightness weaving through trembling cottonwoods. The ranches, however, looked yellowed and parched and made me think of all the golden river bottoms of the West.

Livingston is a railroad and cattle town with an old-fashioned Main Street appeal. Unlike many western towns, like Jackson Hole, which resembles a chamber of commerce movie set, or Aspen, which seems to have attracted half the mediocre actors in Hollywood, there's nothing phony about this place. I liked it the minute I rode in. I ate a breakfast of biscuits and gravy at a cafe that used to serve as the town railroad depot and then got a cheap room at the old hotel where the great film director Sam Peckinpah had lived out his last days.

And then, because it was still early in the morning, I went into the Stockman Bar and had myself a beer. Two guys were slam-shooting eight ball in back. A cowboy walked across the room as if he were wading through tequila. The bartender told me that the summer before she had worked in Anchorage, a town with more saloons per capita than any city in America. I excused myself to use the can and check out the graffiti in the stall, the true anthropological test of a town's character. I liked this place real well. *Here I sit, cheeks a flexin' / just gave birth to another Texan.*

I had another beer and drove back upriver toward Mallard's Rest. The morning was hot and the valley fragrant with the smell of mown hay and cattle shit. The river flowed in channels and winding blue braids, set against a canopy of green cottonwoods and white gravel shelving bars. I ached to fish it.

I followed a dusty switchback down to the river, rigged up and waded out into the lustrous, rushing water. Whitefish began bumping my high-riding hopper pattern. There is a saying out West that no one ever caught a whitefish on purpose. Fortunately these couldn't seem to get their prissy, sucker mouths around the outsized fly. Finally, I began taking a few cutthroats and rainbow hybrids out of a slick just below a riffle where the river streamed over cobbles and tongues of gravel.

These were not the dainty rises. The trout—rainbows and cutthroats—slashed at the hopper with reckless abandon. The cutthroats were a rich golden olive, with the heaviest concentration of spotting running down to the tails. I fished small eddying breaks and cutbank pools in back channels, in the seams between currents and in the holes below the islands. Every now and again, the valley wind kicked up, blowing my casts all over the place and rustling the green canopy of the trees.

The fishing died in the heat and high visibility of noon and I rested in the green shade of a cottonwood, drinking water and eating oranges out of a paper sack. Although the sun was warm, I could feel the first sharp edge to the air, the onset of a high-country autumn. Already a faint dusting of snow lay on the peaks of the Absarokas. In the high passes, aspens were turning yellow in the first nights of hard frost. It would be some time yet before the green cottonwoods along the river began to turn too, but by late September the river would be a blue and golden heartache and the wind would blow mournfully off the cold water into the rustling cottonwoods and willows.

I fished the big water all day, moving upriver and down, as the afternoon stole across warm hayfields and pastures. The black-green edge of evening crept across the valley floor. Lush fields darkened and shadows edged gradually up the pine-thick ridges into the dense understory of the Absarokas. For a time, the broad river was half glare, half shadow. The granite peaks continued to glow a deep alpine blue. My fly disappeared in the circles of an evening rise and I fished steadily until the last light dimmed on the mountaintops and I could no longer see the surface dimpling of whitefish and trout.

I had planned to fish for cutthroats in the Gros Ventre, but in late summer the lower river was pretty much lost to irrigation head gates and ditched to the wealthy ranchers around Jackson Hole. What didn't go to irrigate pasture land was pumped south, along with its choking silts, and flushed into Flat Creek, thoroughly crapping up one of the West's finest spring creeks.

In Wyoming, cattle take precedence over wildlife. I could picture the corporate stockmen now, getting a free ride on the public rangeland and complaining about welfare mothers in Detroit housing projects, then bragging over bourbon-and-branch-water how they were the last self-made men in the West. Still, I'd be a prick too if I ran ten thousand head of cattle in the shadow of the Grand Tetons. I'd be president of the livestock association, wear pointy-toed boots with undershot heels and a gigantic Stetson, drill wells and bulldoze stockponds and poison coyotes with cyanide. I'd patrol my ranch in a Cadillac Eldorado convertible with a steerhorn hood ornament and fly to the capital in my twin-engine Cessna. I'd complain full-time about my tax breaks and run for the state legislature as a big-wheel Wyoming Republican.

Well, better ranches than subdivisions, I suppose. Better ranchers than real estate agents and developers. Better working cattle outfits than trophy homes and toy ranches, or condominiums owned by movie stars, network anchormen and a thousand crooked stockbrokers trading by modem. There wasn't an outfit on the valley floor that could afford to hold out against the developers much longer— at least not the small, family-owned ranches. Pretty hard to sit on a twenty-thousand-dollar acre of ground for the sake of a four-hundred-dollar calf.

I hit the Jackson town square, a kind of hole-in-the-mall western theme park laid out by the chamber of commerce. I strolled down the plank boardwalks, past the antlered arches and rustic, wooden-fronted shops, the cowboy bars that looked like hokey movie sets and the forty tony galleries. Jackson Hole was a hip town full of tourists, working cowboys, trust-funded kids, construction rough-necks, ski bums, petroleum geologists, rock climbers, merchants, white-water boatmen, any number of waitresses and bartenders just killing time until ski season and fly fishermen. Once again I was struck by that popular idea that the West is the place where people go to reinvent themselves.

I had missed the Labor Day crowds and was too early for that annoying promotional stunt known as the Jackson Hole One-Fly Contest. The One-Fly Contest, which takes place over a two-day period during an agony of municipal boosterism, was the godchild of one of the town's better-known fly-shop owners. Not long ago one of his two sporting-goods emporiums burned down in what was of-ficially suspected to be the work of a crazed arsonist. At the time, I was sorely tempted to write a let-ter to the *Jackson Hole News* proposing the establishment of the Jackson One-Match Arson Contest.

Would-be arsonists would team up with celebrity Hollywood firebugs to see who—using a single sul-fur-tipped kitchen match—could burn down the remaining store. (If there is any tackle dealer, fly-fishing school, guide service or overpriced lodge that I have failed to insult by name, I apologize.)

I decided to fish Deadman's Bar on the Snake River, below Pacific Creek. As usual, the Tetons shot up from the valley floor in a spectacular, theatrical mass of pinnacles and peaks, rising above a wide expanse of sagebrush flats, river terraces, dark evergreen forests and gravel outwash plains. That western magnification of the far-off—a combination of high altitude and brilliant sunlight—made the jagged peaks and serrated edges appear closer than they actually were. With each shift in perspective came a change in outline. Groins and crags, not visible before, passed into view or rose unexpectedly above intervening ridges and gaps in the mountain wall. Glaciers and hanging valleys could be seen as the mountain wall opened onto widening chasms that revealed mountains behind mountains and a blue inner core. And in the dazzling air, snow fields gleamed in the defiles and the luster brightened on the high slopes. The peaks in the cluster known as the Cathedral Group managed to stand together and apart simultaneously.

The richness of the Tetons drew closer: radiant forests of spruce and pine, fragrant wildflower meadows, rock outcroppings that shone as though illuminated with an inner light, brawling cascades and alpine lakes, and always the peaks: the peaks filling the morning sky.

I walked the river as I have walked so many before, the air around me smelling of sweet grass and pine. I counted the dimples and circles of rising fish down to a bend where the braided channel flowed past sun-bleached gravel and disappeared behind a grove of willows. The trout were rising to the tiny black-and-white fly called *tricorythodes*. I tied a very small imitation onto what seemed like an impossibly fine tippet and got several strikes but failed to set the hook. Finally I got the rhythm down and managed to take a few trout, none of remarkable size. They were the variety called fine-spotted cutthroat for which the Snake River was famous, all silver and lemony, with bright slashes and brilliant orange fins against a dusting of pepper. They reminded me just a little of harvest trout, the coastal cutthroats found in tidal lagoons in the Pacific Northwest.

I had an absurdly good time; the fish weren't large, but they were beautifully colored and fair fighters. I concentrated on the flow of water and the likely places where trout would hold—in the swirling eddies, along the banks in the side channels and behind boulder stops.

Later I drove down the valley, making the long, winding trek south and across the river, past isolated ranches and the depressing and wholly unnecessary levees that had been put up to protect the town. Below the Wilson Bridge the river broadened out into a bottomland of blue channels and low gravel islands. Here the river was laid out in long, gliding runs and sparkling riffles. Even in the mid-day glare I managed to take a few large cutthroats out of the cutbanks and holes. One was eighteen inches.

The afternoon passed slowly, as time should on a river. The rocks gave up their warmth and shade on the ridges spread into the fluttering aspens. A pale wafer of moon hung in the daylight sky. The flashing line caught the sun and glowed like a burning wire. I fished out the remainder of the afternoon in the fir-scented canyon below where the Hoback and the Snake meet. I fished without a conscious thought, until the evening burned down to the color of wood ash and the green light died in the forest. Later that night the Snake River canyon turned as black as the inside of a crow and there were more stars than I had ever seen in my life.

The next morning the sun broke the crest and again fired the peaks of the Tetons. Dawn, and I was heading over the pass, bound for the Jack Mormon heart of Idaho to fish Silver Creek and maybe visit Hemingway's grave in Ketchum. Later I might roll into the basin above Stanley for cutthroats in the upper Salmon. Or hike into remote Kelly Creek beneath the wall of the Bitterroots. There were arid basins in Oregon still to be seen, shallow antelope valleys and sagebrush plains, and green plateaus rising abruptly from desert floors like miniature versions of Yellowstone. Autumn seemed to lie somewhere just beyond the next range, in a high-altitude wash of blue and golden light. No doubt there would be a washboard road leading to a small coppery creek with no name. The creek would be low, and my fly would drift past cold, sun-bleached rocks and willow-choked bends toward . . . what? Who could say? Like the West, the possibilities seemed endless and I had nothing to lose.

The Surf, The Pines

Thrunk.

Somewhere on the creek bottom, the string on a cello is being plucked: a rhythmic croak coming out of the red canyon. The instrument is loosely strung, but tuned nonetheless to the otherness, the apartness of the desert. Somewhere down in the muck and green-willow smell of the stream, a frog is hitting an A note. Otherwise the canyon seems breathless and still, crystalline and timeless.

The sun beats down upon red Navajo sandstone and umber walls. The acid green leaves of the cottonwoods, responding to even the lightest breeze, stir faintly and then hold perfectly still. Another sound, from the steep pitch of the cliff face: the clear notes of a wren, floating, as though played on a bamboo flute. Eight notes descending the scale, *tee-tee-tee-tee-tew-tew-tew-tew.* Over and over.

The song exaggerates the forenoon stillness. The sluggish desert stream inches forward without so much as a murmur, past tamarisk and willows, passing slowly under the great bridge of rose and ochre sandstone that spans the creek. The world in Natural Bridges National Monument, Utah, is very quiet and very hot—already one hundred degrees in the canyon. On the western horizon, massive cumuli nimbus, great water-bearing clouds, sit like ships at anchor, throwing a collective shadow as huge as Rhode Island.

I take one of the primitive campsites on the rim of the plateau, in the forest of juniper and pinyon pine. I spend most of the day rooting about down in the complex of canyons, exploring the sandstone bridges, hiking the switchbacks. By sundown, great shafts of slanting light pour out of the western sky. Swallows dart in and out of the canyon. A hermit thrush sings far off in the pines. I build a campfire from juniper twigs, as the sun flares and fades and the sky turns rose and lavender. Content, I listen to the crackle of burning juniper and the final twilight cries of birds. Hog-nosed bats flicker about and a wave of darkness rolls westward over the plateau.

Tomorrow I will be in the city of Page, Arizona. The day after, I will be standing in the copper light of the Colorado River, fishing for rainbow trout at the head of the Grand Canyon. Later I'll head for the North Rim high above the desert heat. I'll hike the cool meadows of the Kaibab Plateau, taste sweet mountain air and listen to the wind soughing in the yellow pines.

The embers burn down to soft gray ash. The desert night is chill. I crawl into the down sleeping bag and stare up at a million diamonds in a black sky. I close my eyes. Off in the forest, a nightjar calls: *whip-poor-will*, again and again. I swear I heard this same bird only a few nights ago, feeding on moths in the humid dark of a southern New Jersey forest on the edge of the Pine Barrens, where I once made my home . . .

• • •

I used to live in a small house on seven acres of woods in a tiny rural southern New Jersey township called Estell Manor. Entering town, you set your watch back fifty years. I might still be there today if the rest of the state had met with similar success in holding back the late twentieth century. The township's amateur politicians had a refreshing way of dealing with development—they didn't want any. These good-humored preservationists (they voted to outlaw genetic engineering within their borders before anyone even heard of genetic engineering) were the closest thing I ever saw to Jefferson's dream of democratic freeholders made up of self-reliant farmers, merchants and craftsmen. Today Estell Manor remains mostly trees.

For many years, I worked as a reporter for a morning newspaper in Atlantic City. My beat was simple—I could cover anything I wanted. And so I wrote about Mafia rubouts and crooked politicians and interviewed Santa Claus at the mall (a better interview than the mayor) and covered casino gambling and the cranberry harvest. Once I wrote a story about a chimpanzee named Pancho who was shot after he bit a woman in a bar fight at a terrific but dangerous roadhouse called the Candlelight Tavern. The chimp, dressed in a full-length overcoat, chomped down on the hand of a barfly who tried to swipe his cocktail. ("This was a tragic incident," said the chimp's owner, Margot Lieb, "as it's rare you see a chimp killed for minding his own business and having a cool drink.") Except for the Mafia murders (two dozen and counting), it was all pretty much typical small-town newspaper fare: shallow, vulgar, sometimes unfair, occasionally inaccurate. I couldn't get enough of it.

Occasionally, in search of stories, I'd drive out to the old sand roads, fire towers, iron bogs and abandoned revolutionary war towns of the Pine Barrens, looking for a view of the woods as invented by John McPhee. His slim book, *The Pine Barrens*, was one of those volumes that, like Ross Macdonald's *The Chill* or Jim Harrison's *Legends of the Fall*, kept getting passed around the newsroom until the spines broke and the pages fell out.

On a morning in late spring I followed a botanist into a Pine Barrens bog in search of the threadleaved sundew, a rare carnivorous plant. Another time I spent an afternoon in the company of the police chief of a small pine hamlet (population four hundred) as we drove around the woods checking out mob burial grounds and the dumping sites for torched and stolen cars favored by North Jersey hoods. Once I wrote about the Revolutionary War ghost that still lived in the Green Bank Tavern on the Mullica River. And one October morning, I stood on the edge of a flooded commercial cranberry bog and watched the harvest. A machine beat drowned cranberry vines until a million scarlet beads floated to the top of the bog. The cranberries were raked into shining islands of color and the surface of the water became a performance art piece.

My house lay on the edge of a vast sandy tract of trees, quite close to the border of Cape May County, the southernmost county in New Jersey. I was surrounded by an ocean of pitch pine and black oak, broken only by fields of panic grass and horseweed. In summer the place was lousy with ticks and during hot June nights wood roaches flew out of the trees and covered my window screens. On warm, humid nights the air filled with insects. Whippoorwills would call and I would walk out to the edge of the woods and try to spot their red eyes glowing in the blackness. One such night I woke up around 3:00 A.M. to the sound of a woman being murdered in my backyard. The screams, so human, came from the throat of a rabbit dying in the talons of an owl.

In autumn I might be awakened by what sounded like the baying of hounds. Stepping out on the lawn, I would sight rafts of honking Canada geese, or the smaller snow geese, passing over the Atlantic Flyway. It would be time to duck hunt. In the blue-black dawns Mallards and flocks of whistling pintails wheeled down over the marsh; black ducks muttered in the creek bottoms. We sat numbly in duck blinds, waiting for first light, decoys bobbing in the cold chop. My friend owned a well-camouflaged duckboat and he was something of a fanatic, difficult to hunt with because of his intensity. But he wore the marsh like a skin. He began his season in the heat of late summer, forcing his canoe through flooded reeds and islands of spartina grass, sweat pouring into his eyes, searching for clapper and Virginia rail. Dawn hunting was not my favorite sport, hunkered down in a freezing blind next to my friend's shivering springer spaniel. I preferred hiking through the marshlands at midday, jumping puddle ducks. The shotgun I used was an ancient field-grade L. C. Smith borrowed from a friend, a three-hundred-pound private detective, fatter than TV's Cannon, who no longer hunted for obvious reasons.

The fat detective was an amateur newspaper hound who fancied himself a kind of Deep Throat, but whom we in the newsroom called Jaws. His shotgun was a heavy side-by-side double, and the barrels were slightly pitted with rust. It probably hadn't been fired since Ike's first administration. What

I really wanted was a beautiful little 20-gauge Fox Sterlingworth. It was designed by the brilliant gun maker Ansley Fox, who lived many years ago in the same neighborhood—in fact on the same block— where my friend, the fat detective, now kept a bayside mansion from which he could look out over the coastal plains and see Atlantic City and the lights of his favorite restaurants.

What I liked to hunt for best were the little woodcock that fluttered in from the north as the ground started to freeze in late November. They favored boggy lowlands on the edges of marshes and the soft mast of oak forests. There were two particularly good woodcock coverts near where I lived. Although I never once saw another hunter there, I had no problem following their discarded shell casings. Walking through the woods in early winter, you would kick up woodcock wherever you stepped. The birds paused on the Cape May peninsula before making their migratory flight across Delaware Bay. Worm eaters, their flesh was dark, with a rich, liverish flavor, a taste worth acquiring.

I was the worst wing shot in our group, so it was my job to cook for the two huge celebratory game dinners we held each winter. They were a cross between feast and sacrament. The first was a waterfowl dinner; the second, upland game. The birds were roasted rare in a blazing hot oven. For one upland game dinner I roasted three pheasants stuffed with a hot-chile cornbread dressing; four ruffed grouse roasted in red wine and thyme; a platter of bacon-wrapped quail in white wine and green grapes and half a dozen woodcock flamed in French brandy, served dripping on toast with a jelly made from local beach plums that grew wild in the sand dunes. The homemade red wine on the table came out of oaken casks from the cellars of Italian farmers in Vineland. The vegetables were from local truck farms and backyard garden plots. The only things on the table that weren't shot or grown nearby were the Minnesota wild rice and the after-dinner French cognacs that we downed.

In the Pine Barrens, deer hunting was a fundamentalist religion and the woods in the first week of December were no place for a sane man to be. The pinelands filled with legions of shotgun-toting hunters dressed in Day-Glo orange. Because of the density and closeness of both people and houses, the traditional, high-powered deer rifles were outlawed. Instead hunters carried short-range shotguns loaded with buckshot. In southern New Jersey, there were basically two styles of deer hunting: pot hunting and club style. Pot hunters hid behind trees or crouched high above the ground on crude wooden platforms waiting for deer to pass. Hunters often illegally baited the sites with piles of sweet potatoes. This was a little like stacking hundred-dollar bills on the ground and shooting people when they bent over to pick them up. The club style was even more unpleasant. A drive would be held to flush the deer through the woods. To me, it carried nothing of the mystery and grandeur, none of the solitude and wonderment, of a true hunt. Not that I have ever hunted deer or have any wish to do so. I did, however, once go on a club drive in order to write a newspaper story and, frankly, I found the whole thing was slightly surreal.

It began before dawn. Under a sky darker than the bluing on their shotguns, about twenty-five hunters—badly hung over in the true spirit of woodsmanship—lined up alongside the road near a thicket of pine trees. Their shotguns were mostly pointed at the ground. Somebody's dog barked insanely from a nearby house. A suburban housefrau stuck her head out the window and shouted that the hunters were too close to her property. From somewhere on the other side of the pines, the thin sour notes of a hunting horn rose in the air like the cracking voice of an adolescent boy. The hunters marched into the low blueberry bushes and briars, beating the underbrush and shouting for deer. In the distance, I heard the sound of crashing undergrowth. The forest stood as if transfixed by life and death, predation and slapstick comedy. A startled deer burst from a clump of holly and dashed through the line of hunters before anyone could get off a shot. Throughout the day, this exercise was repeated until someone finally managed to down a buck.

At day's end the hunters marched to the lodge to drink beer, toss back shots of whiskey and devour huge platters of cold cuts. Each year, it seemed a fallen comrade was carted out of a South Jersey deer camp, stricken with a heart attack. Few were ever shot.

Although I don't hunt deer, I'll eat venison any chance I get. And so when a friend of mine from the newspaper called me one winter evening to say that his father-in-law had left him a saddle of fresh venison from a "road kill" (Pineys regard game laws in much the same way Neapolitans observe traffic lights), I wasted little time driving over to his house. A saddle of venison is a cut similar to a standing rib of beef. I crushed juniper berries and rubbed them into the tenderized meat. The venison, basted in herbs and wine and laid over a bed of sliced onions and root vegetables, was roasted in a blazing oven for precisely one hour. When it came out, the buttery meat from the center was a perfect rosy hue. I made a sauce with the pan drippings and red wine. It was one of the five greatest meals of my life.

Jacklighting deer was a time-honored custom in the pines and I never met a hunter who wouldn't accept venison taken out of season. The poaching seemed to have little effect on the overall deer population. They were like rats with antlers. There were more deer in New Jersey than in the Maine woods. So many, in fact, that in crowded suburbs like Princeton you could kill deer just by driving your car to work in the morning. Everyone who lived in the woods had a story about how they almost clobbered one on the way home from a favorite tavern. The mayor of Atlantic City killed a deer while driving back from his bribery trial. Once I almost hit one on my way to the appropriately named Buck Tavern, where, ironically, I was about to enjoy a venison dinner, a good story that has—as my source, the fat detective, liked to say—the added advantage of being true. Often I would see deer cross my yard and melt into the woods or hear their hooves clicking on my gravel drive.

After a good winter storm, I would often see their tracks in the fresh snow, along with the prints of raccoons circling my garbage cans. Once I saw what I took to be the prints of a fox. They were smaller than my neighbor's dogs, which had free run of my yard. I knew there were plenty of gray foxes in the woods. Driving on the back roads of the pines you would often see their gray hides stretched out over the doors of cabins, looking remarkably like flying squirrels. Trapping was a passion in the Pine Barrens and not everyone did it for pin money. One of my editors, who came from a long line of Pineys, and who I figured was pulling down about fifty grand a year in salary, never missed a season's trapping. It's in the genes, he explained. He later moved to the North Carolina low country, which is said to be remarkably like the Jersey pinelands. I never saw the appeal of trapping; Pineys who were really into it routinely had themselves inoculated for rabies protection.

Jersey winters were brutal and springs came hard and slow. My cure for cabin fever was the Five Points Tavern on the edge of Vineland. They served venison sausage on Super Bowl Sunday and good Italian food all year round. You could watch TV all afternoon and at the end of the day the barmaid would count the dead soldiers piled on the bar and tell you what you owed.

If you wanted to get some fresh air, you drove out to Richland to hunt for roadside barbecue. A man called the Kingfish cooked over trash barrels near the railroad tracks. I used to buy ribs and quarts of something he called Louisiana pork stew. The Kingfish walked with a limp that he had received from a blown truck tire. The legal settlement had left him a millionaire.

By early March I'd find myself driving around the pines looking at tea-colored cedar streams and shallow opaque lakes. There were no trout in Pine Barrens rivers, the water being too tannic. And dark as ink too, a mixture of iron-rich groundwater and tannins coming off Atlantic white cedars that lined the banks. Near my house was a shallow impoundment fringed by pines called Maple Lake. Early in the season, I'd spend many hours there with a fly rod, a chorus of spring peepers croaking in the background. Small, starving pickerel would charge out of the waterweeds and rip into the fly. The few I kept were impossible to fillet, having an intricate and puzzling bone structure even more complex than shad. I poached them whole in white wine, lemon and butter but they still came out tasting like the bottom of the lake. It was like eating a plate of tadpoles and dragonflies.

The lake was quite beautiful, though, as long as you didn't stare too hard at the trash that lined the banks. It always astonished me to learn how far Jerseyites were willing to journey—in this case to the middle of the boondocks—just to discard a Big Mac wrapper or take off a condom. No matter how far I would wander into the South Jersey pine forests, I was constantly kicking up trash. On cross-country car trips, it struck me how the highway litter dramatically declined the farther west one got from New Jersey and Pennsylvania. By Indiana, the roadsides were so clean you imagined you were in another century.

Few of nature's colors are more extravagant than an eastern forest in the yellow green of springtime. By May the pinelands were blooming like a miniature Appalachia. All light looked new. And then the leaves on the oaks and maples darkened to deeper summer shades and the first heat waves left the forest panting. The air itched with hay fever. On weekends a long stream of cars poured out of the pines heading for the Jersey Shore.

I followed the old Tuckahoe Road out to Marmora. Here the winding tannin creeks spread out into brackish marshland. Red-winged blackbirds flitted in and out of freshwater cattails and swaying reed grass. Soon the flowering spike grass of the higher marshland appeared and I was driving over a causeway above islands of salt hay and cord grass. The marsh, flooded by tides twice a day, was as green as the fairway on a golf course; by fall the sod banks would turn as tawny as a lion's hide. The Jersey Shore is really a string of barrier islands, sand ridges that rise slightly above high tide and parallel the true shore of the mainland. These islands are separated from the mainland by huge tidal basins slowly filling up with marshes richer than the greenest Iowa cornfields. Rum runners used to ship their cargo through the maze of blue inlets. And over the years other criminals have found uses for the coastal waterway. I had a friend whose two older teenage brothers once set fire to the Longport Water Works, burning it to the ground. They escaped by swimming across an inlet under cover of darkness, forever earning themselves a place in the Teenage Hall of Fame.

I'd pull into the sand lot at Corson's Inlet at the south end of Ocean City. The dunes would be bursting with sea rocket and golden rod. I'd string up the big fly rod and hike through the maze of sand dunes and beach grass, swatting at green-head flies. Climbing out at last over the ridge of the primary dunes, I would feel the stiff breeze of the Atlantic full in my face. It was impossible to cast into the surf through a head wind so I hiked south to the huge sand spit at the end of the island. Here the tide raced around Corson's Inlet, creating ribbed bars and shallow trenches. One time while fishing the Strathmere side of it, something seized my fly with more power than any fish I had ever encountered, with the exception of tarpon in the Florida Keys. The reel handle spun so wildly it skinned my knuckles and blood ran down my wrist into the salt water.

The fish burned up the drag on the cheap Pflueger. And then whatever was on the end of that line threw the hook. It might have been a shark. But I like to imagine it was a yellowfin tuna, a pelagic fish gone drastically off course. Incredible as it sounds, a yellowfin tuna had been taken by a bank fisherman on the inlet sands at the north end of Ocean City earlier that summer. Such a fish would have made me a legend on the fly rod. I could have gotten my name in my own newspaper. It was odd, but for all the times I had gone to Corson's Inlet to fish for blues and stripers—any South Jersey beach, for that matter—not once had I seen another fisherman with a fly rod.

My best day at Corson's Inlet came on a humid evening in mid-June. The surfcasters had left with the falling light, leaving me the run of the beach. I waded into the chop near the mouth, cast and felt something bump my surface fly. I picked up and cast again and immediately the popping fly disappeared and my rod bent under a solid but living weight. A bluefish jumped twice and then shook itself on the bottom, rubbing the line into the sand. By now I had noticed that the water around me seemed to be trembling with terrific agitation. What looked like a cloud of sand passed under me and then rose to the surface like a scattering of silver confetti. It was a swarm of fleeing baitfish. Gulls dropped from the sky by the tens and twenties. Bluefish crashed the bait ten feet from the beach.

I waded to shore to avoid being bitten. Abruptly my fish came off and I reeled in and tied on another fly. I was using a monofilament leader instead of a wire shock tippet and the sharp teeth of the bluefish had sheared it off. I made another cast and immediately drew up tight on another bluefish. I got about five minutes of play out of this one before it too sheared off the leader. For the next twenty minutes I cast and cast again, tying on new flies with trembling fingers, until the wolf pack passed through the inlet out to sea, the gulls following in a wheeling mass. I had hooked fifteen bluefish—one on each cast—beaching only two. My twelve-foot leader had been bitten down to six inches. I carried the pair back to the parking lot and filleted them on the spot, flinging the skeletons into the dunes. A humid bank of thunderclouds rolled in. Lightning flickered. Driving home, I baked the bluefish Genoa style—with potatoes, parsley, olive oil, garlic. Outside my house the forest appeared mothlike, dim as spiderwebbing. Then the thunder let go with a tremendous crack and the treetops plunged in the wind. Powerful gusts tossed the branches, turning up the pale undersides of leaves. My backyard dimmed one moment, brightened the next, as bolts sizzled over the treetops. The rain hit the roof like a burst of BBs. The meat of the bluefish cooked up white as snow and I ate it staring out the window.

Without the shore towns, summers would have been unendurable. For a time before I lived in the Pine Barrens I rented a small apartment on Absecon Island in a community called Downbeach right next to Atlantic City. My apartment was one block from the beach, and just another block from the bay, so hurricanes were always highly interesting. As a would-be sportsman, I learned how to fly-fish for stripers on the bay seawall at Longport on the southern tip of Absecon Island. I figured out how to time my backcasts to avoid passing cars.

The best fishing was at night; stripers were attracted to the pools of light cast by street lamps. Longport was my favorite "downbeach" town. Its mayor was a dapper, snowy-haired bachelor who favored dark navy suits and polka-dot bow ties, took his whiskey neat and made his real living as a pool shark, hustling games in the private Bay Club in Margate. He lived in a small apartment over the Betty Bacharach Home, a rehabilitation hospital for disabled children, and had been mayor for a hundred years. Longport also had Lenny's beachfront hot dog stand, which was the place to go after the bars closed at four in the morning. Best hot dogs I ever tasted, even better than Nathan's in Coney Island. Adjacent to Lenny's was a wonderfully silly tourist attraction called Lucy the Elephant, a giant stuffed pachyderm that stood as high as a three-story house. Lucy always reminded me of the wooden elephant in Victor Hugo's *Les Misérables*, the deserted statue the Parisian street kids made into their home. On truly oppressive summer nights, when the humidity was thick enough to drink, I would eat a couple of Lenny's hot dogs and then go for a midnight swim off my beach. If there was an offshore wind, I might fly-fish in the black surf. There was a 10:00 P.M. beach curfew, but the Ventnor cops never bothered me. It felt eerie casting into the black breakers and it was hard to see the stars. The mercury vapor lights over Atlantic City turned the night sky the color of Pepto-Bismol. Even after I moved to the Pines I would stare into the black eastern horizon and spot the obscene halo.

One day a state senator, who was also a friend, asked me whether I thought that a certain big-wheel developer with the usual great plans for Atlantic City had—as the saying goes—"sand in his shoes." It was a common expression, used to describe a person whose heart would never leave the Jersey Shore. And for all that repelled me about New Jersey in general, and Atlantic City in particular, I always thought that I too had sand in my shoes. But I was wrong.

One August I returned from a western trout-fishing vacation. It was so hot, the white sky above the Pines looked like it was covered with lint. A pall of carbon monoxide hung above the mini-malls, housing tracts and the new subdivisions. Jellyfish were washing up in the shore towns, along with medical waste, hypodermic needles and an unusually high number of dead dolphins. My newspaper ran countless articles about why Flipper was dying. Even the whippoorwills in my forest sounded wheezy and sick.

Needing groceries, I went down to my local general store in the Pines. I had known the owner for six years—I think I can honestly say that we were friends. The first thing he did was take my credit card and run the numbers through his verification machine like crap through a short dog. Not once out West, while I was among strangers, had anyone bothered to look up the balance on my account to see if I was ripping them off. I began to see my friend's behavior as a metaphor for the Garden State. And so I made it official. Rather abruptly, I quit my job and moved out West.

I have not been back to South Jersey, not even to visit. I have no desire to. But occasionally, when I am camped out at the bottom of a desert canyon, or hiking a steep Sierra slope, or curled up inside a sleeping bag within sound of a salmon river, I swear I can hear the surf.

High Sierra

I left San Francisco at midmorning, the skyline still covered in a late-lifting October fog. It was going to be a hot one—the haze would burn off by noon. At the Bay Bridge, I rolled up behind a phalanx of outlaw bikers, their open denim jackets flapping in the breeze, their bored-out, heavy-duty Harleys passing over the steel span in a burst of thunder. Funny how you never saw bikers smiling as they rode in formation. White-trash descendants of Dustbowl Okies who blew in out of the Central Valley. Successful crank dealers, though—good heads for business. The Hell's Angels had incorporated and their logo was a registered trademark. I followed in the slipstream, losing them somewhere around San Leandro. Traffic moved eastward in a majestic, toll-free trance. The center lane ticked by and the East Bay disappeared in my rear-view mirror. It was going to be a fine day, speed traps and the California Highway Patrol notwithstanding. I was making it my business to be in the Sierra Nevada Mountains by sundown. For tax purposes, it was a business trip.

Trucks swept past with a blast of hot air, the clang of the big rigs vibrating in the wind. Autumn—it still felt like summer. I raced through the Castro Valley and Livermore, where the dry hills seemed ready to burst into flame at any moment. Drought and wildfire alerts. I tried to imagine tangerine flames licking at the hills, burning up the subdivisions. Live oaks managed to grow in the fumey atmosphere of a freeway interchange.

Soon suburban tract homes were giving way to California surrealism. At Altamont Pass, windmills shaped like airplane propellers spun on empty hillsides like bad conceptual art. Just beyond the pass, the freeway dropped into an agricultural theme park as flat as a billiard table. At the little town of Manteca, things slowed down and the highway narrowed to two asphalt lanes baking in the sun. Hand-lettered signs appeared on roadsides offering fruit, cider, bags of almonds. The locals pronounced them *"am'nds."* They called cement *"cee-ment"* too, but this was no John Steinbeck novel. Tractors drifted back and forth endlessly along the furrows of the crop-dusted fields. The ag-towns were concrete shopping marts, their centers flooded with Mexican stoop laborers. Diesel smog hung in the air, mixing with dust and herbicides. I passed stainless-steel barns the size of blimp hangars, aqueducts evaporating in the hundred-degree heat and acre upon acre of bulldozed earth. Pistons banged along river embankments and snake-like siphons sent water purling into endless rows of crops. The industrial odor came as a shock.

Heat shimmered the valley. I popped open a beer just in case I fainted before I got to the mountains. Gradually the valley floor rose and I was climbing into the foothills, past Gold Country towns with forty-niner place names like Knight's Ferry and Chinese Camp. I chose the right fork toward Yosemite and eventually came upon a blue canyon reservoir dotted with pleasure boats. The road ascended steadily into ponderosa pines and the forest released a hot, resinous smell. A little higher, and the pines started giving way to mixed conifers. The coolness of the Sierra announced itself. I passed shady resort campgrounds offering cabin rentals, crossroads stores that sold gas and beer and picture-postcard lakes that I glimpsed briefly through the pines.

Bare granite peaks appeared in the distance. At a hairpin curve, I gazed down into a canyon of digger pines and glimpsed the Tuolumne River coiling along the bottom of the gorge. Once I had driven down there on a dirt "road" that was like something out of the journals of Lewis and Clark. But the fishing was good. I remember the colors more than the trout. The gold and copper of canyon water, the rapids, white and green, the riffles with their amber bottoms, the black shade pools by the trees, and, at sundown, a river that poured like hammered silver.

At Yosemite, I encountered more traffic than I would have thought likely for a weekday in late October. I ate my lunch sitting on a warm rock in the middle of a sun-drenched meadow. No picnic tables for me. A Steller's jay climbed a pine tree, hopping from branch to branch without moving its wings.

Back on the Tioga Road, I headed for the highest paved mountain pass in California. The Tuolumne River appeared again on my left, this time as a high western meadow stream that meandered peacefully through fawn-colored fields surrounded by whitish lava domes, bare granite outcroppings and pointed minarets. The smaller Dana Fork coiled around, bounced over flat runs, its riffles sparkling. I spotted a gray-crowned rosy finch, the so-called high-altitude "refrigerator bird." And a horned lark. Hikers crossed the meadows for a trip down to Waterwheel Falls in the Grand

Canyon of the Tuolumne. At this altitude, the sun was a white radiance in a sky so blue it suggested infinity. I went over the mountain pass in second gear, at an ear-popping 9,945 feet above sea level. And then the Sierra roof seemed to drop out from under me and I was staring down into the shimmering wastes, sun-baked ridges and waterless valleys.

Western junipers, corkscrewed and weathered, were scattered across the landscape like living driftwood. A great cascade of sagebrush rolled out from the hills. Directly below me was Lee Vining Creek. The steep walls were covered in stands of aspen and belts of Jeffrey pine. The aspens, like the cottonwoods along the creek, were aflame with autumn.

I headed south, past spooky Mono Lake, the Sierra looming on my right. For a time I drove alongside an exquisite roadside creek lined with brassy willows and cottonwoods. The cased fly rod in the backseat hummed like a tuning fork. I tasted sage and juniper. By the time I reached Hot Creek, the eastern wall of the Sierra had thrown a silhouette of violet over the valley and the desert basin seemed to radiate ground heat back into the cold twilight.

Hot Creek made a few serpentine loops through a stark western meadow and then flowed into a shallow gorge of rough lava outcroppings. It was a narrow stream, filled with chara weeds and complicated currents. Clear spring water poured over pea-sized gravel and brown trout rose in the fading light to suck insects from the surface.

I tied on a tiny sedge fly and aimed my casts to fall somewhere between undulating waterweeds. After a while, a trout rose to my fly in a limpid swirl and my rod bowed under its pull. It was a brown trout, as vivid in its spawning colors as Saturday night in New Orleans. The evening sky in the west burned down to the color of wood ashes and a nighthawk, coming out of a dive and opening its wings, made a sound like a small sonic boom.

The sun rose hard and white out of Nevada, lighting the granite wall of the Sierra. The escarpment shone in desert air clean enough to rinse the lungs. I rolled out of the sleeping bag and stretched in the cold dawn glow. At the resort town of Mammoth Lakes, a clerk in a sporting-goods shop suggested I fish the middle fork of the San Joaquin River, which he described as a kind of mountain necklace set down in the Sierra pines.

I followed the asphalt road over the crest and dropped once again into the western drainage. The switchback road descended fifteen hundred feet into a forest of firs and lodgepole pines. White-barked aspen stood out in patches against the darker conifers and when the breeze stirred, the delicate aspens shivered. Their hiss suggested falling water. The day was outrageous, even by High Sierra standards. Nature can provide some truly radiant scenes. There is the golden green an Appalachian spring; the fathomless blue of Lake Tahoe; the sun-burnt redness of desert canyons; the claret stain of a cranberry harvest in the New Jersey Pine Barrens. And quaking aspens, their flame gold leaves set against a Western sky.

Because I am a good tourist, I stopped first at Devil's Postpile National Monument to observe one of the world's larger collections of vertical basalt columns. Standing sixty feet above a pile of rubble, the six-sided columns resembled pipes rising from a giant church organ. When I realized the lava rocks weren't going to play a toccata and fugue in D minor, I seized my fly rod and hiked down to Rainbow Falls. The steep waterfall sounded like faraway applause. A continuous spray rose from the base, charging the air with negative ions. Even my blood felt carbonated.

I had planned to spend a morning on the middle fork of the San Joaquin. I was tempted to spend years. The middle fork was a mountain jewel flowing over dark stones, past tangled logjams and deadfalls. The water was low but very cold. I flicked casts into the shade. The solitude was invaded only by bird calls, the low mutter of the stream and the wind rustling in the pine boughs. Sunlight fell through the spaces between the trees, leaving bright patches of on the forest floor.

The fork was full of trout that rose to a dry fly and I caught a half-dozen rainbows in a morning's leisurely fishing. They were all wild—small but very firm from the cold water, and with that compact, blocky feeling so characteristic of rainbow trout.

I returned up the switchback road, leaving behind the forests and granite domes of the canyon. The car ground in second gear going up Minaret Summit. Over the pass, descending once again into the valley of the rain shadow, the air was sharp with sage and bitterbrush. In Long Valley the Owens River made winding loops through a shortgrass Western meadow. To the east lay the wastes of Nevada; at my back, the granite peaks of the Sierra, jagged cordillera of light.

The river unwound. Up close, the water was glassine, transparent as a spring creek. Here and there along the banks were fly fishermen making picture-perfect casts against a towering mountain backdrop. At any moment, I expected someone to launch into a commercial for beer or Toyota Land Cruisers.

An elderly gent huffed across the meadow, fly rod in hand. He introduced himself as a retired cataract surgeon from San Luis Obispo. Said he came out every spring and fall to fish the Owens and Hot Creek. The browns, he explained, had come up from Crowley Lake to spawn and were hiding under the sweeping, undercut banks. Allowed as how he'd taken a few. "Better get down there before the wind starts blowing," he advised.

The river flowed south under the spell of gravity, its motion built into it by the composition of the earth upstream, and down. I stepped into the water and felt the urging of the current at my legs. The sensation of moving water is always a little eerie and profound, and with it comes the feeling I often have at the moment just before sleep, of losing consciousness, of being drawn irresistibly toward an unknown ledge. I walked the grass banks, looking futilely for insects on the surface. No matter, I tied on a generic caddis, on the assumption that trout are our friends and will take whatever we give them, a theory I plan to publish someday in *Scientific American*. My line was rolling out. The stream poured over fine river gravels and I was alert for the bubble trails of trout.

The afternoon wind that the doctor had warned me about was kicking up. Long Valley, like the entire eastern Sierra, is famous for its weird convections, upper-air disturbances and sudden lightning strikes. Everything looked peaceful, though, the clouds sailing overhead as white as gulls. The stone face of the range transformed itself with each hour of shifting light.

I picked my casts carefully, and every now and again a rainbow would part the water and snatch my fly. I stared into refracted light and waving chara blooms and eventually made out the form of a two-pound brown trout. Perfection. The wing tip of the jet airliner passing overhead in a thin contrail could not possibly be as fine or aerodynamically sound as the dorsal fin on that trout. I crouched down for the all-important low profile and tied on a heavily weighted nymph, a technique about as pleasurable as arc welding. But it brought my fly down to the fish and suddenly the line made a wonderful ripping sound in the water, a sound a fishing companion once described—to the utter consternation of his wife—as the tearing of silk panties. In the finest tradition of hook-and-bullet pornography, I dragged this "hawg" onto the bank. The rather prosaic term "brown trout" hardly does justice to the coloration and fine detailing. The trout I landed was covered in a mantle of jet-black spots and its belly was like butter melting into a stack of wheatcakes.

Clouds massed in the west and their shadows traveled slowly across the grass. Now and again I'd look up from my fishing and gaze out at the hills, covered in knots of green juniper, or at the towering granite wall of the Sierra escarpment and pretend I was having deep philosophical thoughts. One thought I did have was just how lucky it was that Los Angeles had cheated the valley out of this beautiful river so long ago. Of all the western water battles, few are more haunting than the plunder of the Owens Valley by the city of Los Angeles during the early part of this century. Municipal water managers maneuvered the farmers out of their riverfronts and water rights. In a backhanded way, L.A. did the place a favor. The theft spared the arid valley the insult of relentless growth and the nonstop subdivision of land that has consumed the rest of Southern California. This place was so empty it was practically a national park.

There followed a week of Indian summer, and then the mercury dropped in the throat of the thermometer. The breezes stirred off the cold stones of Convict Creek and I could feel winter in the dying rustle of the cottonwoods.

An upper-air disturbance was forming over the valley, shockingly cold. I headed north, and as I climbed a mountain pass above a belt of Jeffrey pines, I thought I smelled burning clutch plate. At one hairpin curve, I almost skidded out of control, imagining for a moment the fireball my car would make as it sailed into a pine copse. But I came out of the skid all right, secure in my belief that nothing truly bad can ever happen to a man who owed as much on his credit cards as I did.

Descending into the valley of the West Walker River, I was reminded once again how much the ranch country here resembled Montana. California might lie on the other side of the mountains—but this was the West. Shining mobile homes and aluminum trailers appeared at the edges of irrigated pastures. Willow-choked creeks ran through backyards or raced down stony juniper terraces. The river swept northward under blowing cottonwoods, past rangeland and open cordilleras and magnificent boles of ponderosa pine. I could see Nevada in the distance under a bank of storm clouds. The desire to get out of my car and fish to the state line had a terrific appeal. Maybe I could cross the desert in my waders, hike all the way to Las Vegas. Or Reno, another small town with a big electric bill. I could tromp into the lobby of the MGM Grand, holding a fly rod and a stringer of dead trout, and no one would even look up from the slot machines.

I rigged up under a cottonwood, choosing a gold-ribbed hare's ear, and stepped into the achingly beautiful stream. Cottonwood leaves fell on the water like petals in a Chinese poem. I saw something flash deep within the pocket water, as if someone were signaling from below with a hand mirror. A nymphing trout. I worked the tiny nymph deep, the sun low on the glittering water. There was an electric tug on the end of my line and I came up tight on a rainbow. It made two aerial twists and darted for deep cover. I maintained a delicate tension just below some imaginary breaking point that I had calculated for the two-pound test tippet, and soon I was turning the trout over in my hand.

I took two hearty browns out of a run where the river poured over a mottled bottom. Fifteen yards downstream a shallow riffle deepened into a greenish slot. Here the river pressed hard against a high bank of cheatgrass and gnarled juniper. The run felt right but I came up snake eyes.

Now the river poured down a small plunge pool, creating a vertical column of starry bubbles. Out of this effervescence a fluid ribbon of opulent water poured onto a smooth, deep run that ran for twenty yards. Trout rose to the tongue of visible current, enjoying tiny olive mayflies in the washout.

I know *baetis* when I see them. I dug into my fly box and took out the smallest olive emerger I could find, tied this onto a nearly invisible strand of 6X tippet and dropped the fly into a seam between the faster current and the slower water. Trout rose above and below my fly. I picked up and cast again. This time the fly disappeared down the hole of a trout ring. A strike. For some seconds, the fish held steady in the current against my bending rod. And then it made a churning run for freedom. Twice I eased it toward the shallows, and twice it darted off. But at last I managed to guide the exhausted fish to the bank and pick up the yellow trout in my hand. I measured it against the rod—seventeen inches. I couldn't have been more pleased with myself if I had been Ernest Hemingway.

I continued to cast until some shift in the barometric pressure signaled an end to the fishing. The valley discharged its light and the temperature plunged by degrees. A black, majestic cloudmass formed over the eastern basin, casting a huge shadow. It was late autumn in the high country and snow would be falling soon on the mountain passes. I could feel the day shutting down and, with it, the season. It was time to go home. If I hurried, I might make it over Sonora Pass before the storm.

His Own Private Idaho

Perhaps the most practical bit of advice Ernest Hemingway ever gave to American writers (other than don't ever try to fire a shotgun with your toes, ha ha) was that all good stories mention three things: the time, the place and the weather.

Landscapes, the sea, the quality of the light . . . fishing for trout . . . drinking red wine chilled in a spring in the Spanish countryside . . . hunting animals, making love, facing war. . . . These were the things he wrote about best. By the time he had returned to the remote Idaho mountain town of Ketchum, to hunker down in his final days, neither the writing nor the living was going particularly well.

I once knew a character in Atlantic City who claimed he had fished with Hemingway in Sun Valley shortly before Papa committed suicide. It is remarkable how many people claim to have known the author. Doing some quick math in my head, I figured this man would have been around thirteen years old at the time of Hemingway's death. Being a trained journalist, I knew how to ask sharp questions.

"Did he look depressed?" I asked.

"We were all depressed," the man said.

Hunter Thompson once wrote that Ketchum was Hemingway's Big Two-Hearted River. By this Thompson meant that Hemingway pretty much knew his good years were over and that the world he was once able to see "clear and as a whole" had changed. But there was still the tiny mountain out-back of Ketchum, his last good country. Here the mountain air had a freshness like his very best prose, the kind he used to write when he was in total control of American English. Hemingway was free to fish in the Big Wood River that flowed past his house or hunt ducks and pheasants in the fall. In his last days, the author was a gaunt figure, often seen walking alone over stubble fields, shotgun in hand, or drinking with rugged townspeople in the Tram, the Alpine or the Sawtooth Club. He had found, as we might say now, his own private Idaho.

He was the century's most famous author. But at the time of his death, as well known and pop-ular as he was, Ernest Hemingway no longer exerted the kind of influence he once had on American writers or writing in general. Faulkner, an author he had overshadowed, was now seen to be vastly su-perior. And then there was the machismo, that cult of hypermasculinity, the unfortunate posturing of a pretentious, albeit truly brave, man.

Hemingway could be an overbearing megalomaniac, but that scarcely dismisses twenty or so short stories and *The Sun Also Rises*. Certainly not the scenes where Jake Barnes and his friends cross the Pyrenees into Spain and fish for trout in that cold river and witness the running of the bulls at the festival in Pamplona. Certainly not "The Snows of Kilimanjaro," with the hyena prowling on the edge of the camp and the final airplane ride toward that blinding white snowfield on the mountain. Certainly not "Big Two-Hearted River," where Nick Adams, injured from the war, gazes down into a Michigan stream and sees trout motionless above the gravel in a rising mist of water and sand.

I was not of that generation in awe of Hemingway. But I have to confess that when I rode into Sun Valley to fish Silver Creek for the first time, I knew I had to visit Hemingway's grave before I ever wet a line.

I found the old Hemingway house, one of those modest faux chalets with a pair of elk horns hanging over the doorway. At least I *think* it was his house, the one he had bought from Bob Topping for fifty thousand dollars back in 1959. It looked out over two bends in the Big Wood River, which was deep in cottonwoods and stands of aspen, and it had views of two mountain ranges, including the jagged peaks of the Sawtooths to the north. His grave was about a mile away, in the cemetery at the north end of town, lying in the shadow of the ski run on Mount Baldy. Nearby stood the headstone of Hemingway's great friend, Taylor "Beartracks" Williams, Sun Valley's chief hunting guide, to whom the author had given the original manuscript of *For Whom the Bell Tolls*, and whom he helped to bury. "The world is a fine place," Hemingway wrote in that novel, "and worth the fighting for and I hate very much to leave it."

I drove down the valley of the Big Wood River, past the little towns of Hailey (birthplace of Ezra Pound) and Bellevue and out to Picabo and Silver Creek. Irrigation sprinklers sprayed a fine mist into the barley fields. The air had a special dry clarity, a little like a desert, an aridity that put brilliance in the light and in the wind-polished hills.

147

In order to fish the Silver Creek Preserve, you have to first sign the registration book in the Nature Conservancy cabin. I signed myself in as Harry Morgan of Key West. I rigged up, walked down to the willow banks and stared into the spring creek; it was clear enough to read *The Portable Hemingway* in. The creek flowed by transparent, its smooth surface reflecting the cloudless Idaho sky as it wound slowly through a luxuriant valley bottomland beneath pale, chalk-colored hills. Tiny mayflies were sprinkled over the current, and here and there were the rings of rising trout. There seemed to be two types of mayflies coming off the water at once, the yellowish *ephemerella infrequens*, which are called Pale Morning Duns, and some smaller mayflies with darker olive bodies.

I tied on an imitation of the smaller of the two mayflies, because this is usually what fishing authorities recommend, and began casting, throwing big, showy S-curves into my line to get a drag-free drift on a current so smooth it would show every mistake in technique. After a while, a big rainbow pulled my fly down and, in a burst of speed, ran line off into a bed of watercress. I lost the fish in the tangle.

This kind of fussy spring-creek fishing was not Ernest Hemingway's cup of Mount Gay rum. He preferred the faster waters of the Big Wood River. Silver Creek is properly the domain of his eldest son, Jack, who makes his home in Sun Valley and who spurred the Nature Conservancy into buying up the Sun Valley Ranch along the creek, creating the preserve. Not that he's a fanatic or anything, but as a soldier Jack Hemingway once parachuted behind enemy lines in Nazi-occupied France with a fly rod strapped to his pack. He is fond of saying that he spent the first fifty years of his life being the son of a famous father and is now spending the final fifty years being the father of famous daughters, Margaux and Mariel. But I think that he will be deservedly remembered for helping to save Silver Creek.

The hatch of mayflies gradually subsided and it seemed as if someone had turned off the trout rings. I changed flies, seeing if I might interest a trout in a small red ant. The creek glided over rich wavering beds of watercress and elodea. Blackbirds flitted in and out of tules rising above the banks. I tried imagining what the sparse sagebrush and cottonwood country around here looked like when Hemingway first came out in the autumn of 1939.

It was the tycoon Averell Harriman who had lured Hemingway to Sun Valley. At the time, Harriman was trying to run his Union Pacific Railroad and get Americans interested in a little-known European sport called skiing. Harriman dispatched his friend the Austrian count Felix Schaffgotsch to comb the mountains of the West in search of the perfect spot for a deluxe ski resort. The count found it in the middle of nowhere—a sun-drenched, snow-filled Idaho valley next to an old mining town called Ketchum.

Harriman wasted little time constructing a lodge in the remote mountain outback, accessible only by Union Pacific train. He commissioned his railroad engineers to design the world's first chairlift, patterned after lifts used to haul cargo onto banana boats. Hollywood luminaries, high society and the Eastern establishment flocked to the slopes. But Harriman needed to convince the public that Sun

Valley was a year-round resort, offering world-class fishing in summer and hunting in the fall. It was then that his publicist hatched the brilliant scheme to hire Ernest Hemingway as Sun Valley's writer in residence.

The deal was a sweet one. Hemingway and his family got free run of the Sun Valley Lodge in exchange for allowing themselves to be photographed at play in the great outdoors. Most of the time, the author would be left alone in Suite 206 to finish writing *For Whom the Bell Tolls*. Whatever initial reservations Hemingway had about this publicity stunt, they were soon dispelled by the glorious duck and pheasant hunting he found in the creek sloughs and barley fields. In no time, Hemingway was playing roulette at the casinos in Ketchum, duck shooting with new friends Gary and Rocky Cooper and raising hell in the bars. One of his favorites was the Alpine and he thought highly of its 6:00 A.M. happy hour when all drinks were poured free of charge so manly imbibers could get a jump on their day. When Hemingway's third wife, Martha Gellhorn, left the lodge that first fall to cover the war in Finland for *Colliers*, he promptly converted Suite 206 into a gambling den for his evening craps and poker games. His nine-year-old son, Gig, ran up a six-hundred-dollar bill in his first month there, beating the record held by the Aga Khan's kid, signing for trap and skeet-shooting lessons and ordering up flaming shish kebab and guinea hen under glass. Of all the splendid photos taken by the lodge photographer, Lloyd "Pappy" Arnold, perhaps the finest is his classic portrait of Hemingway seated at the typewriter in shirtsleeves. Who knows, perhaps someday I too will be hired as a writer in residence at some fabulous theme resort—probably Marine World or the Mystery Spot in Santa Cruz.

The water bulged and swirled around my floating ant. I raised the rod and came up tight on a medium-sized rainbow. The trout's colors were as bright and clean as an Idaho morning.

The round, wind-polished Picabo hills change each hour passing from a pale straw to a buff suede. Idaho literally means dawn. "Ea dah how"—Shoshone for "sun comes down the mountain" or, "It is morning."

Hemingway loved Silver Creek, but it was the ducks he was after, not the trout. There were rafts of them, pintails and mallards, thousands floating in the marshes, feeder streams and sloughs, hiding in the ditches of the irrigated ranch land. His favorite way to hunt them was sitting in the bow of a canoe gliding down Silver Creek. He wrote to his son Jack that he had never seen so many large, rising trout and he compared the creek's remarkable clarity to that of a British chalk stream. I tried to picture what the creek must have looked like to Hemingway on those autumn mornings, the air crystal still, the satin creek reflecting rust and carmine willows under an endless expanse of blue.

For safety, only the person sitting in the bow of a canoe hunted. Hemingway's friend, Gene Van Guilder, the young Midwesterner who ran publicity for Sun Valley Lodge, was killed by a friend's careless shotgun blast while floating Silver Creek for ducks. Biographer Carlos Baker related how Hemingway delivered the graveside eulogy for the young Van Guilder, who died intestate with only seventeen cents in his bank account. His widow insisted on burying him with his expensive hunting gear. Which led Hemingway to mutter to Pappy Arnold, as the two were leaving the cemetery, that they probably should be grateful she hadn't thrown in the fishing rods and frying pans, too.

And then there were the October pheasant hunts. Shotguns booming over the sagebrush hills in the golden afternoon light. Mountain quail and chukar flushing on hillsides scented with sage. Cock pheasants rising out of stubble fields and cackling in the aspen groves. It all must have had the quality of a Hemingway short story, where everything is informed at once by both life and death.

The creek sighed as it passed along the willows. In the air above the glasslike water, thousands of tiny *tricorythodes* flies had gathered for a grand mating swarm. An infinite number of black and white specks spun and shimmered in the morning light. I tied on a tiny black fly with snow white wings. Soon a swarm of spent insects would be fluttering down on Silver Creek.

Wherever Hemingway went, people followed. To Sun Valley. To Key West. To Spain. It was as if he single-handedly propped up the tourist economies of any number of small towns, ports and villages. Each summer Key West holds "Hemingway Days" during which paunchy, middle-aged drunks grow white beards and compete to see who can best capture that Old-Man-and-the-Sea look. Likewise, every summer TV-news crews dutifully arrive in Pamplona, Spain, for the running of the bulls; for one week each summer reckless young men in white shirts and scarlet neckerchiefs race for their lives down narrow streets one step ahead of the horns.

Some have said (wrongly) that Hemingway's public life was his crowning artistic achievement. It *was* exciting. He embraced life with such enormous zest, and sought out experience at any cost, that he changed the rules of the game for all time and enlarged the world. But I suspect that what continues to draw people to his towering example, what drew me to his grave in Ketchum, was something found only in his words. At his best, Hemingway wrote a prose no writer before or since has been able to. His sentences flowed. Something occurred at every level, above and below the current. He created scenes of such accuracy and intensity as to be like actual life experiences for the reader. Can anyone conceive of a book with more *living* in it than *The Sun Also Rises*? Has there ever been a more acutely observed rendering of the natural world than "Big Two-Hearted River"?

The spinners settled onto the creek and trout rose everywhere. For the next half-hour, I hooked and released fish as spinners drifted downstream and feeding trout made rings on the water.

The good years ran out and somewhere along the way, Hemingway lost his *lucha por la vida*. With his body wracked by alcoholism, injury and disease, his liver as big as a salmon, he idled in Sun Valley, a kind of wraith. He was so seized with paranoia that he actually believed the FBI was spying on him. (Incredibly, we now know from documents released under the Freedom of Information Act that the FBI *was* investigating Hemingway, that its agents had gone so far as to secretly debrief Hemingway's doctors at the Mayo Clinic, where he was being treated for psychiatric disorders. Proving only, I suppose, that J. Edgar Hoover was even crazier than Hemingway.)

On and off in the last years, Hemingway had worked to complete the manuscript of *A Moveable Feast*, the memoir he had written earlier about his expatriate days in twenties Paris. Reliving those memories, his prose had some of the vigor and luster of his youth.

But the renewal of strength was short-lived. One bright morning in early July of 1961, as the Idaho sunshine fell in warm pools onto the living-room floor of his Ketchum home, Ernest Hemingway unboxed a double-barreled, pigeon-grade Boss shotgun, and—for reasons that no doubt must have felt entirely appropriate to him—he pressed both barrels against his forehead and tripped the trigger. He was sixty-one years old.

I left the preserve to fish downstream at the prairie meadow below Point of Rocks. And I had some good fishing for brown trout there late in the afternoon. Afterward I returned to fish out the evening on the Nature Conservancy water.

The hills had turned a watermelon pink in the failing light. To the north were the peaks of the great mountain range. The air was clear and still. As I cast to the last of the rising trout, I thought about how, in this lifetime anyway, the physical world is all any of us can ever really hope to know.

Winter Steelhead

When you make the decision to become a serious steelhead fisherman, and you live in Northern California as I do, then you had better resign yourself to fishing in the wintertime with the cold and the rain in your face. This is not a sport for sissies.

A friend of mine has claimed that winter steelhead fishing actually increases the libido. Early on I discovered that while this was not necessarily true, I would still need a big rod.

When I first moved to California, I discovered that the better steelhead fishing—indeed just about all steelhead fishing—took place in winter when the big rainbow trout came back from the Pacific to spawn. If I wanted to pursue summer-run steelhead within earshot of a crystal rapids, with the sunshine releasing the perfume of wild blackberries into the air, then I had better move to Oregon.

In California the real thing didn't even begin until late November. On the Russian River, my home stream, this kind of fishing often took place in a seemingly stationary landscape of cold fog and river mist relieved by brilliant afternoons when the sun struck the redwoods at an oblique angle.

At dawn I would walk out into a static world of twisted oaks and heavy winter grasses, the river polished to a dark, antlerlike sheen. The valley air was scented with woodsmoke. Houses along the river, set back in a tangle of trees and ferns, appeared dim and indistinct when viewed through a curtain of fog and drizzle. That absence of light in the morning fog suggested other absences that translated into an undefined but sharply felt melancholy. Among other things, I wondered how people living along the riverbanks could stand the eternal damp and mildew.

Often the land was covered in a clinging ground mist known as a valley fog. Fly lines disappeared into the vapor. A pale sun burned weakly behind the haze, and the cold and dampness penetrated everything.

Farther upstream lay wine country and I discovered vineyards filled with shining yellow mustard grass. There were great flocks of starlings in the fields and deer browsed in the bottomland, their coats full and lustrous. I cast into bank shadows, my line backlit by a sun sinking into bare willows and poplars.

It was a big river, flowing more than a hundred miles through a broad pastoral valley of vineyards, dark redwood groves in the lower reaches and gentle Pacific dairy farms in its final, widening stretches. If the sandbar at the mouth was open, salmon began entering around late September or early October. By Thanksgiving steelhead were showing up in the lower river. Although by all accounts the fishing once was epic, old fishermen describe the present-day river valley more as a museum or ruined mausoleum. I must have made a thousand casts before I caught my first Russian River steelhead.

But they were there: in the shallow Austin Riffle and in the pool known as Watson's Log. At a place called Freezeout and near the redwood groves above the Wohler Bridge. At Oddfellows Park and in the green, shadowy banks behind the Foppiano Vineyard.

Yet these fish were not enough. Because the Russian River was so tame, so domesticated, its fishing never quite satisfied. And so after the first good rains of winter, I would find myself making the long ride up the coast to the little town of Gualala.

The Gualala River, located a hundred miles north of San Francisco on the Mendocino border, was in many ways typical of California's shorter coastal streams. But in another more meaningful sense, it was one of a kind and priceless. I first saw the river canyon on a mild winter afternoon with the sunlight filtering down into a grove of redwoods. The river was the chalky green color steelhead anglers love.

Each bend in the canyon held a curving bar of sand and gravel on one side and a deep green pool, bulging against steep rocks, on the opposite bank. When rain raised the level of the river, steelhead entered from the tidal lagoon. As the river dropped and cleared, the pools under the redwood trees began to freshen or "green up." When the pools turned to just the right shade of light, green, when I could almost see my wading boots on the bottom of the river, then the steelhead seemed to strike freely. But as the days passed and the level of the river continued to drop, the pools turned emerald, and the steelhead, feeling less secure, seemed disinclined to take a fly and would instead often slide down into the deeper corners of the pools. When it was extremely low, you could sometimes stand on a high bank, look down into one of these refulgent pools and see dozens of steelhead bunched up on the bottom. This up-and-down cycle of the river was repeated with each rainfall. After heavy rains, the river ran light brown for several days (there had been altogether too much logging in the hills) before changing back to that soft inviting shade of green.

Steelhead used the rain-swollen river to swim up into the shallower spawning tributaries. Later in the season, I would hike into the upper canyon and see steelhead paired off on shallow gravel beds. The backs of the trout were spotted like river stones, so that at first I couldn't see them, only their rippling shadows.

Everyone fished the slow, green pools of the lower river with sinking lines. The trick was to work the fly directly at the level of the fish. A trout's metabolism slowed down considerably in colder water, so winter steelhead weren't likely to move very far to take a fly. The depth the fish held at and the speed of the river determined whether I needed a moderate or a fast-sinking line. On the slower pools of the Gualala, I noticed that the more successful anglers fished their flies as deeply as possible without actually snagging bottom, all the while managing a natural drift. By avoiding drag—that is, the pull of a fly against the current—the feathered offerings passed through the pools at the same speed as the current.

On the gravel bars, I heard a good deal of esoteric talk about flies "breathing" underwater and saw any number of interesting, fanciful patterns. Much later on I figured out all one pretty much needed to know about steelhead flies: when the river was high and cloudy, one used larger, fairly buoyant flies with good silhouettes; when the river was low and clear, one used smaller, more subdued flies and lightened the leader. Just how light was relative. The average size of a Gualala River steelhead was about eight pounds, but I saw fish taken out of the river that easily could have gone up to fifteen pounds.

I discovered that winter steelhead generally favored the lower ends of the pools. When the river was prime, they held in the shallow tailouts, in the slight dip at the bottom where the water began to break over the lip of a pool. It always surprised me whenever I would find big fish in shallow water. But such was the case. Only when the pools dropped and the water became exceptionally clear would steelhead seek the safety of the deeper water.

The Gualala pools had a certain local fame and fanciful names taken from nineteenth-century logging operations. At early morning, I found the better fishing to be at the lower end of the wide gravel bar known as Switchvale. Later I would cross upstream and fish the pool where the north fork entered the river. Steelhead waited for the river to rise so they could ascend the tributary and spawn. In the evenings, steelhead in the lower end of Miner Hole grew restless. At any time a steelhead might erupt against the surface of the green pool and shatter the stillness. And during evening high tides, rollers often were spotted at the very wide pool known as Mill Bend, just below the Highway 1 bridge.

These broad pools called for long casts. This meant heavy lines that could turn a fly over smoothly at great distances. In some quarters it had become fashionable for fly fishermen to try and take steelhead on extremely lightweight wands. Watching a steelhead twist one of these insubstantial rods into a pretzel one morning made me think of a friend who refused to eat nouvelle cuisine on the grounds that it was toy food. Light rods were for *trout*.

The deep, slow pools of the Gualala not only called for long casts, they demanded smooth presentations. There were no ruffled surfaces to hide a blown cast or dampen a line slapping the water.

Another thing I was told to expect was that winter steelhead have a very soft take. It seemed a contradiction. Yet when the giant fish mouthed a fly, often the only thing one felt on the end of the line was a slight hesitation or pull. More often than not for me, these hesitations translated into bottom snagging. After a while, my heart no longer leapt each time I hooked a weed or nicked a stone.

A typical day of steelheading at Gualala might begin at Sonoma County Park on the south bank. Here a path disappeared into the perfectly diffused light of the redwoods and led down to a sun-drenched gravel bar at the foot of Miner Hole. After fishing through the splendid lower pool and tail-out, I would hike upstream along the wide gravel bar, my breath condensing in the cold, and ford the river below Thompson Hole. If it was early afternoon, the deep water bulging against the south bank would be catching the first shadows, so chances of hooking a steelhead were greatly improved. At midstream, a submerged redwood stump created a barely visible surface wake. Here steelhead rested in the lee of the log. The tailout also was superb.

From Thompson's I might ford the stream once again and proceed upriver to Donkey or the Snag Hole. Or I could make the long trek back to Miner Hole in time to catch late-afternoon shadows sliding off the north bank. Now the sun would be holding at a low angle and much of the river would be stuck in glare. This would gradually subside and with luck, steelhead would start rolling within the looming shadow of the lower pool. It would fish well into evening.

Later, standing on the gravel bar at dusk, talking with the other fishermen, I might see a moon-rise over the redwoods, one of nature's more indelible moments. It was often set in a twilight so blue and perfectly still as to feel warm, despite the bitter night. I could easily work up religious feelings about those evenings in the canyon.

But the best fishing of all generally took place in the grayish light of dawn. I would set out from the coastal town of Gualala under a brooding headland darkness, surf crashing against the sandbar at the end of the lagoon, sea wind blowing into the cypress breaks. Some mornings the gravel bar at Switchvale resembled a parking lot; other mornings it was eerily deserted. Often I would join a gaunt-let of anglers who had materialized out of the gray dimness. The steelhead were fresh from the ocean and hadn't been in the river long enough to be spooked. They were massing there for the big run up the north fork tributary.

One particular dawn, standing in the lower pool at Switchvale and shaking with cold, I noticed a nervous agitation in the shallow water directly upstream. I watched as a steelhead slipped in over the lip of the pool. A soft drizzle began and pretty soon the steeply forested canyon filled with a heavier down-pour. Steelhead were moving into the pool under the cover of the rain. I felt a slight tug at the end of my line and I brought the rod up sharply on a boiling trout. I lost that steelhead and blew two more hookups.

In the turbulent light of the rainstorm, the mysterious inner life of the canyon was revealed in moss and lichen gleaming on the rock face and in the pale undersides of leaves kicked up by the wind. From steeply rising banks, a thicket of ferns and tangled underbrush receded into the rain and permanent darkness of the redwoods.

I remember another dawn at Switchvale, fly lines slicing over the pool in the first glimmer of morning. The angler beside me came up on a steelhead so large and powerful it took a full twenty minutes to land. The fish was as bright as a bar of silver and I could see the sea lice on its flanks.

And then there was that time at the lower end of Miner Hole, the pool obscured by shadow. Four or five of us were swinging our lines through the best water. Toward the later part of the afternoon something began to happen. It was as if someone had thrown on a wall switch. I can't explain it. Out of nowhere, a steelhead slapped the surface. We heard the guttural explosion and stared at the rings, widening and disappearing on the water. An angler below me covered the fish with a long, almost heroic cast. His line drew forward and he pulled up tight on the steelhead. It was a fish of about ten pounds and when it was beached I saw a faint lateral scarring, as if it had once struggled in a trawler's net. Intermittently steelhead began to roll throughout the pool.

With trembling fingers, I worked a wind knot out of my tippet and tied on a small black-and-green fly. A steelhead rolled above me and I waded upstream to cover the fish. My line swung through the steelhead's lie, and when it drew forward I brought the rod up, sharp. It came as a great surprise, as all steelhead do. It was like hooking a log that suddenly came to life. The steelhead thrashed at the end of the line and led me down the pool for fifteen minutes. I managed to beach it. It was a hen fish of about seven pounds, silver and rose. As it lay gasping and quivering on the stones of the gravel bar, I saw that its dorsal fin had been rubbed smooth. A hatchery fish? It was as bright as a winter moon.

Another angler had a fish on downstream, but it unhooked itself almost at once. Other fishermen stepped into the stream. There seemed to be a hierarchy to the pool, with the better fly fishermen crowding the lower end. And then, as abruptly as it began, the pool turned off. I don't know how else to describe it. I fished until dark without further luck and walked back under the black redwoods to the car. That night in the bar at the old Gualala Hotel, the conversation centered on just how fine everything had been. I remember thinking to myself that night: Well, I guess I'm a steelhead fisherman.

I learned an awful lot that first winter on the Gualala. That the fishing could be slow but the canyon magnificent, full of meaning beyond its obvious beauty. I have fished many other steelhead rivers since. But when my mind turns to winter steelhead fishing, I think first of the Gualala. It's one of the few things I'm sentimental about. This river taught me everything I know.

Firehole Days

By autumn the fishing has begun to change in much of the Mountain West. There will be one or two snowfalls that melt by noon, followed by bluebird skies and candy-colored light. Now the breeze stirring off the water tends to come as a bit of a shock. And cottonwoods are dropping their leaves along the banks of spangled rivers.

Outside Ketchum, the hills around Silver Creek are continually reshaped by a clear dry light. Idaho is either the beginning of the Pacific Northwest or the end of the Rocky Mountains, depending on how you view these things. Towns and rivers are named after silver mines and Pacific salmon. A chill wind comes down the pass.

Except for the spring creeks, dry-fly fishing is over. On the bigger rivers, brown trout have moved onto their spawning beds, and to get to them you have to wade out deep into the current where`the gravel washes treacherously under your cleats. But the browns are deeply colored and have taken on a rich, glowing patina, like the portraits of saints, and fishing always seems best when there is so little of it left.

I head east across the lava flats and high desert. On the outskirts of Arco, bird hunters strike out into arid sagebrush, and the distant crump of shotguns is in the hills. To the newcomer, the landscape is startling, and the heart can fill.

Now the road climbs slowly out of desert prairies unspoiled by tourists, and in the distance the pale, jagged outline of the Grand Tetons appears dimly across the Snake River plains, the least appreciated but most fascinating view of these mountains. Gradually the dry terrain gives way to lush haystack valleys and forests of lodgepole pine. Briefly I consider fishing the Harriman Ranch, with its knee-deep meadow grasses and nesting sandhill cranes. The Henry's Fork of the Snake River at Last Chance, Idaho, is all I ever imagined the West could be. But I head on for Targhee Pass and the Yellowstone Plateau.

I want to fish the Firehole River; it has been some years since I last stood on its banks. I want to go back badly enough not to care how time, tourism and a major forest fire have recast it. I want to see the river as I saw it as a young man. Few memories are as evocative as those autumns I spent on the Firehole. This is where I taught myself how to fish for trout.

Plumes of steam rise from the geyser field, drifting upward into the cold autumn air. I carry rod and pack through pine copses stinking of sulfur, past the bleached skeletons of downed trees. At Biscuit Basin, the Firehole ripples with fluid life. It is meadow water here, a virtual spring creek, full of wavering chara beds and streaming elodea. The trout are flawless, lounging at the edge of light patches, turning water and sunlight into sentience.

The pools are like wavering refractive lenses and at first the mottled trout are completely in-visible against a bottom of fine gravel and black volcanic sand. But they are there, the faintest glim-merings. I look for shifting olive shadows in the water.

But the Firehole trout choose not to rise or show themselves in any meaningful way. I tie on the most supple, the longest leader I can fashion and drift a small olive emerger into the clear, streaming windowpane. The weedbeds, in their many shades of green, shift mysteriously in the currents, their motion bewitching. I wait in vain for fabled insect hatches to come off, as they say, "like clockwork" and trigger a rise.

The river makes several serpentine loops through deep-cut channels and grassy banks and then disappears behind a screen of pines and springhead bogs. The valley narrows to a crossing between two plateaus favored by elk and grizzly bears. The lodgepole pines are thick and sunlight plays on the surface of the river, casting reflections like gold coins over the black lava bottom.

The riverbed is black rhyolite; there are spots where the crust is so thin you can actually feel thermal heat from hot ground springs radiating up and through your waders. Farther downstream the western bank is rimed with calcified salts and a whitewash of sinter, the residue of hydrothermal dis-charge. Geysers and hot springs belch constantly into the river, their steam rising over the valley like a thousand smoke plumes. Surely this is the most outlandish trout stream on earth.

The Firehole River actually was discovered not by trappers in the early 1800s, as is commonly supposed, but in September 1979, by me, on a bleak overcast morning in Yellowstone National Park. I was looking for a river to sit beside while I ate my lunch. To an easterner, Wyoming came as something of a jolt. In the bunchgrass meadows at Fountain Flats, buffalo stood in the pale, cold light, their breath rising in steam, snow flurries falling onto their dark backs. It was still summer, but only if you judged by a calendar. The river that day had a dull metallic surface that made it hard to see into and the trout were rising to tiny brown sedges. Sulfurous plumes drifted ghostlike above the lodgepoles, and along the banks steam escaped from vents in the earth. Scalding water bubbled up from miniature pools and poured into the cold aerated river.

The fishing that first day could charitably be called problematic. The sedge flies rode and fluttered down currents made overly complicated by weedbeds, potholes and lava outcrops. I had nothing in my fly box to match the dark skittering caddises that floated off the river. Success seemed to hinge on intangibles.

Frustrated, I headed upriver to the riffle water above the billowing steam of the Midway Geyser Basin. Here was trout water I could understand. I fished a small nymph through the bouncing riffles and soon began catching twelve-inch rainbows. They were so beautiful I never quite got used to them.

Just above this stretch lay a polished oxbow in the river called Muleshoe Bend. It was bordered by a high roadside bluff; a smoking cavern lay like a dragon across its tail. Its lower meadow was guarded by a fifty-foot cauldron that burped and spat. Muleshoe Bend looked pretty, but it was the most surreal and complicated piece of dry-fly water I had ever seen. Because of the weedbeds, its currents were as confused as oil on water. The current looked lazy, yet sped by. Every trout lie became a riddle wrapped in the enigma of the water.

So I remained in the easy riffle where I continued to catch trout. And in the bitter chill of evening, when the fishing was done, I stood for a long moment watching geyser steam billowing above the snow meadow, and listened to the hollow, mournful bugling of elk. I thought to myself, not for the first time that day: Here is a life worth living.

I couldn't get enough of the Firehole. More than just the feeling of pleasure at being in a beautiful place, this river made me pause. I felt myself at a beginning.

At the time, I knew jack about fly fishing. I was entirely self-taught. I had none of the right flies; knew nothing about streamside entomology or fly tying. Even to this day, the fisherman's vise is not what I allude to when I speak of the pleasures of tying one on. I knew little about trout behavior or stream life. Hell, I could barely cast. Yet when I saw the Firehole, I wanted to make it my own.

The following day the snow melted, a phenomenon I would grow accustomed to on the Yellowstone Plateau. At a sunlit bend in the river beside the geyser spring known as Ojo Caliente, an old gentleman showed me how to coax up brown trout by drifting small olive mayfly imitations between the weedbeds. If the hatches became too complicated, I could always fish hopper imitations in the meadow stretches, like the one near Goose and Feather lakes. The sun-drenched meadow there was a banquet for the senses. It was well off the road and to get to it you strolled through a lodgepole forest, past tangled deadfalls and bleached, skeletal pines. Here a lukewarm bog seeped into the river where it meandered through the buffalo grass. For a few weeks the hopper fishing was fabulous until too many nights of hoarfrost killed off the meadow's terrestrial insects.

I met Cecil, my first trout bum, while fishing the weedy channels at Lodgepole Bend below Ojo Caliente. Cecil was a Chicago cab driver when he worked, which was seldom. He drank cheap Gallo Chablis from a coffee mug, never beer, and he fished with a rod of flamed bamboo. "Break it, you buy it," he said, as he handed it over for me to flex. He had been variously sleeping in his truck, living in a teepee and mooching off a girlfriend in Casper, Wyoming. He led me up Sentinel Creek above the Firehole and we caught brook trout in that clear, cold tributary. He taught me how to call down elk, and he drew me a map of the Railroad Ranch water over in Idaho. "Only time I ever envied a man for his property," he said, presumably referring to the late Averell Harriman and his Union Pacific Railroad holding.

At West Yellowstone I hooked up with a young man named Matt, a college grad who apparently had majored in beer and coeds. He was enjoying his last spell of freedom before going back to North Carolina to go into the family business. Matt had driven to Yellowstone by way of Texas (to see a girl he had once met briefly) and he was going to fish for a week and then hunt birds in the Canadian Rockies. Together we drove down to Idaho and hiked into the remote Bechler River in the extreme south-

169

western corner of the park. When we failed to trick the Bechler rainbows into taking our hopper flies, we threaded live grasshoppers onto bare hooks, all quite illegal because bait fishing is outlawed in the park. Matt managed to hook one of trophy size and almost fell into the river as he made a lunging dive when, at the last moment, the trout came unhooked. On his final day in the park, we fished the Firehole at a swift staircase of broken channels and plunge pools that held both rainbows and browns. I recognized it even then as far too good a stretch of river for the general public. After all, I was a purist now.

On the Firehole, I assumed a state of hypnotic concentration known to fly fishermen, where I would look up after hours of focused fishing only to realize the day had fled and it was time to break down the rod. Gradually I came to figure out the insect hatches well enough to begin taking trout out of the slower, trickier stretches like Muleshoe Bend and Biscuit Basin and the streaming weedbeds at Ojo Caliente. Sometimes it was enough just to stick the rod tip into the water and feel the life of the river.

I gradually discovered that the bigger trout favored lies close to the grassy banks. Rainbows seemed to prefer the faster, more aerated water; the browns were found in the slower channels, where the current glided with easy deliberation over the black rhyolite bottom. The autumn spawning colors of the brown trout were wonderful.

When small caddis or mayflies settled onto the water surface, trout would rise from the fountain moss and trailing elodea and the insects would disappear in little blinks that widened into swirling rings. I was captivated by the gossamer world of the mayflies.

The river made a kind of musical slurping sound as it passed through the meadows and under the lodgepole pines. But farther downstream, beyond its forest stretch known as the Broads, the Firehole paused at the brink of one last deep pool before rushing headlong into a canyon of dark volcanic rock. On this white-water cascade the din rose and fell like the cheering over an athletic field.

At Firehole Falls, the sustained hammering was like a great wind blowing in the crowns of the trees. Curiously, I never saw anyone fishing the final half-mile of the river below the falls. It seemed a likely spot, though. Here the Firehole and Gibbon River joined together in a lovely bunchgrass meadow to form the Madison, which flowed out of the park all the way to the Missouri. One night a guide who I met in the Frontier Bar in West Yellowstone, explained to me that if I just took the time to fish a streamer fly or a giant stone-fly nymph below the falls of the Firehole, I stood a pretty good chance of catching some of the best brown trout of the season. They ran up from the Madison River to spawn in autumn and were brought up short at the foot of the falls.

But that first September, I took my largest Firehole brown near Goose Lake Meadows. Here the river flowed in sweeping bends past springy bogs, over weedbeds and rhyolite. I let the fly, a high-riding hopper imitation, drift as close as possible to the undercut bank. I never saw the trout rise. The fly just halted in middrift and went under as though sucked into a vacuum. My line sliced past me, the reel shrieking. The brown trout thrashed wildly downstream and burrowed under a bed of potamogeton. I could feel the very sheerness of the line against the weedbed; I could count the knots in my leader as it caught and vibrated on the mossy tufts. Somehow the frail tippet held. And when the brown trout eventually surrendered, I measured it at eighteen inches.

. . .

On a particularly bitter, wet afternoon, when the threat of snow lay heavy on the air, I was fishing the sweep of river known as the Fountain Flats, just above Nez Percé Creek. Steam rose from meadow fumaroles and escaped out of cracks in the crusted riverbank. The pines beyond looked dark and fertile. A deep, funnel-shaped pool lay at the bottom of this stretch of water, and when I floated a tan caddis over its lip, the fly was seized with such astonishing violence that the tippet came apart instantly. Yet I barely felt any weight behind the take, it was all over that fast. Later there were the usual unreliable reports about a brown trout of mythological size being caught in that pool.

Whenever possible I liked to end the fishing day at Midway Geyser Basin, watching the steam plume in the cold air. The small rainbow trout were easy to catch. Often, after releasing a trout back into the riffles, I would wade to the bank and kneel over one of the hot springs, rubbing my freezing hands to restore circulation. An ounce of pale sun might show behind the billowing steam. With the shortness of the autumn day, twilight quickly transferred itself onto the gray and white sinter of the geyser field. If snow lay on the ground, it was a bluish coat. Elk were in rut and their evening trumpeting was so beautiful it raised gooseflesh. The elk were wearing their rich winter coats and their breath steamed in the air, like the hot springs.

Often I fished with a small dry fly called an Elk Hair caddis, which is tied from the rump hairs of the mooselike deer, and I was delighted by the perfect symmetry of things.

At night, back in town where I had a room, the air over West Yellowstone filled with the comforting tang of woodsmoke. The stars hung like ice crystals above the cabins. Every cafe had at least one snapshot of the building buried up to its eaves in snow. Just to let you know how things stood in winter, in case you were thinking about moving here. Despite the tourism, the town had a largely unreconstructed feel to it. An outsized trout or elk mount hung on the wall of just about every shop in town. For all I knew, they taught taxidermy in the grade school. It was easy to spot the many fishing guides hanging around West Yellowstone; they were the ones who looked like Zen frontiersman.

At the bar in the Stagecoach Inn, I met a guide named Skip who told me he held a master's in philosophy from the University of Colorado at Boulder; that suited him perfectly for rowing a boat. Skip had a day off, so the next morning (guides always fish on their day off) the two of us hiked down into the Firehole Canyon. If we stared hard enough into the white-water uproar we might glimpse the dull green flash of a nymphing rainbow trout. They slashed hungrily at our large Bitch Creek nymphs and we could barely contain them in the cascading water.

But I preferred the slower meadow stretches; this water seemed to better suit my mood. At Biscuit Basin, in the gentle glide of the meadow, I learned about "masking hatches." Caddises were on the water and fish were rising, but not to the visible flies. Squinting into the surface film, I noticed what seemed to be tiny midges riding alongside the sedge flies. Though smaller, they were more numerous;

the trout were responding to the greater biomass on the water. Naturally I didn't have anything in my fly box to match what they were taking. But the point is, I figured the problem out myself. Hot damn— I was on my way to becoming a real fly fisherman.

In the high blue chill of October, the fishing got even better. When other streams in the park were slowing down, the Firehole remained a constant. There were days when the surface of the water was covered with the tiny olive *baetis* flies and the fish were rising everywhere. This was attributed to the many springheads and hydrothermal discharges that in cold weather stabilized the river's temperatures. In summer it was an indifferent fishing stream, much too warm, and many trout sought sanctuary in the colder feeder creeks. But the snap of a Yellowstone autumn brought the Firehole's insects and trout to life.

At Midway Geyser Basin, where the steaming spillage from the geyser known as Excelsior poured into the river over an escutcheon of white sinter and orange algae-covered rock, trout fed just inches away from currents that could parboil them alive. When the mountain man John Colter first told people he had seen a river hissing steam, with springs hot enough to cook its trout, no one had believed him. I did. Riverside geysers were always erupting without warning and hitting me with boiling droplets of wind-carried water.

Naturally I visited other rivers, inside the park, and outside, too. A long float trip on the Yellowstone River in Paradise Valley in Montana. A hike well up into the sagebrush and bison valley of the Lamar River for cutthroat. And I landed and released the largest brown trout of my life on an evening on the Madison River at a place that locals called the Back of the Barns. But always returned to the Firehole.

By late October, Yellowstone was virtually empty. In the pale buffalo-grass basins, bison by the hundreds gathered. Huge billows of steam rose out of fumaroles and smoking geysers, in some places obscuring the river. Often I would stop my fishing and simply stare at the buffalo standing so silently in the falling snow, their vaporous breath rising with the steam from the hot springs.

All throughout that first autumn, the Firehole rippled in my dreams. And each autumn after that I came back. And then there was a break, a period of years where I no longer returned to the Rocky Mountains in the fall, when I felt there were other things I had to do in my life.

Now I am back. The weedy currents slide over ledge rock, past outcroppings and the crusted embankment. There is a chill. To get here, I rode across gray mountain passes, down through evergreen valleys riddled with the snows of early autumn. I had a mild trepidation that to see the river again would be a little too much like psychoanalysis. Yet the Firehole seems exactly the way I left it. Although, I know this cannot possibly be true. For one thing, there are more anglers this autumn than there were in the past; we seem to bristle at the sight of one another even as we nod. At the moment no trout are dimpling on the smooth currents, on the lambent surface of the water. But the brown trout are poised along the weedbeds, and every now and again a trout will sidle into the weeds and turn to reach a hidden cress bug. The conventional wisdom is that one doesn't even bother fishing Muleshoe Bend on the Firehole unless there is a hatch on. But I can't resist. As a fisherman, I remain wholly unreconstructed. Watching the currents pass over streaming chara and wavering ranunculus is as hypnotic as staring into a fire.

So I thread an Elk Hair caddis onto a gossamer leader, squeeze it dry, lengthen my cast and drop it into the river's fluid meander. I feel the drag of memory on the fly. I yield to its pull and surrender.

Letter From
Out West

Dear Jim:

In your letter you asked if I could give you some idea of where to fish on your first trip out West. I suggest you come out in very late summer or fall. The fishing is slow then and the crowds will have thinned out. Pack light: a rod, your gear, a few good books.

The first river you'll want to see is Silver Creek, and who can blame you? Notice how the hills around the creek seem constantly to change under a dry coloring light. Wind and light define everything out here. The light of Idaho needn't fill just the sky—it can fill your mind, even your life.

This is the kind of magical spring-creek water you've been reading about in all the fly-fishing books, its currents as confusing as hell. I agree it is the loveliest water to look at and not as hard to fish as you might think. It's late in the summer, so the insects are going to be very small. Each morning you should see a spinner full of tiny black-and-white flies called *tricorythodes*. I use the Greek here because I know you are tough and can take it.

Get a room in Hailey, it's cheaper there. Or camp out at a KOA.

MICHAEL CHECCHIO

At night, hang out in Ketchum and Sun Valley. Visit the Alpine Bar and the Tram where Hemingway used to drink. Don't bother driving up Trail Creek to see the monument; it's for tourists. Instead, find his grave in the Ketchum Cemetery—it's in the shade of the ski slopes—and plant some old-fashioned fly, say a Royal Coachman, in the dirt.

At night you will feel the weather change. This is the onset of a high country autumn. Fall starts in late August in the Mountain West. There will be one or two nights of hard frost and the leaves of the aspens will begin to change. One day you will look up at a high mountain pass and see a strip of golden flame. On clear nights, the stars will look like salt poured into a coal black frying pan.

After several days you should have exhausted your interest in Silver Creek. Now is the time to hike out to the desert sinkholes and prairie streams. Be sure to see the Big Lost River, if only for its name's sake.

Now head east into the lodgepole pines. You are going to fish the Railroad Ranch on the Henry's Fork. Jim, if you could create a river in your mind this would be it. The Railroad Ranch is *everything* you ever hoped the West could be. By now the glamor insect hatches will be over and you'll have the place to yourself.

Get some beer and grub in Last Chance and pack it into the stream. Never mind the water near the road, pretty though it may be. Hike in over the immense meadow that leads down to the ranch. For a cheap thrill, look behind you at the pale serrations of the Grand Tetons floating in the distance. Enjoy the quietude. Watch for long-billed curlews and nesting sandhill cranes. You can hear the loud rattling croak of the cranes a half-mile away. When you finally get to the meadow river—it will be a twenty-minute walk—with luck you should see rainbow trout rising everywhere to glittering Pale Morning Duns and Blue Wing Olives. How we are taken with the sparkling life of the mayfly. The idea of a beautiful, diaphanous insect that lives for a single day, only to make love and die, seems to touch us directly. *Ars longa, vita brevis* and all that.

Never mind. You never liked to match the hatch. Tie on a small cinnamon ant or find the tiniest black beetle in your box and fish it near the banks. Try to resist all those surface rings made by rising trout in the middle of the stream. The truly big rainbows are lying against the embankments; look for their bubble trails. I know this sounds incongruous but the biggest trout always seem to leave the smallest feeding mark on the surface. Every now and then look up from your fishing to stare at Sawtell Peak and pretend you are a well-published lyric poet. Fish until the ranch cabins are backlit and the sun slips behind the green shadow of the pines. Be quiet and *listen* to the evening star.

You will want to linger here for days and watch the meadow drink up the light. But it's time to move on. At Last Chance the road leads north to Yellowstone. Ignore it for now. Find the dirt road by Henry's Lake that will lead you over Red Rock Pass and into Montana's Centennial Valley. This is unspoiled ranch country and the hay fields along the Red Rock River are stacked with a thousand golden bales.

Fish the brushy, willow-lined Beaverhead for some of the biggest brown trout in Montana. At Dillon, check out Poindexter Slough, one of those fussy spring creeks. Try the Big Hole River in its rich hay valley. And then go upriver into its pure, clean headwaters and try to catch some of the last grayling in Montana.

Keep heading north into the Bitterroots; follow the trail of Chief Joseph and the fleeing Nez Percé. Walk the battlefield where Colonel Gibbon's cavalry tried to massacre the sleeping Indians at dawn. Remember how Looking Glass turned the battle around and how Colonel Gibbon took a bullet to the crotch (good shot!).

Above all, fish the Bitterroot River. Here in the narrow mountain valley you will come across a perfect little Montana town called Hamilton. This is a long shot, but see if you can find a copy of an out-of-print book called *John Medicine Wolf*. It was written by a hip young Indian living in Hamilton, Michael Moon, and is a kind of regional cult classic. I'm always on the lookout for a copy. If you find it, I'll reimburse you.

Follow the Bitterroot down into Missoula. This is a great western university town just crammed with good writers. The literacy rate is so high it's disturbing. Missoula becomes "Meriwether" in Jim Crumley's detective novels; remember anything can happen here. This is a town of good bars and drug deals, so you should feel right at home. The late Dick Hugo taught in town and wrote some of his best poems here. No, I don't know if the Milltown Union Bar (Laundromat & Cafe) is still standing. But I understand why you want to see the wonderful saloon Dick Hugo wrote about so beautifully, with its orphan wars and bad cowboy painting over the back bar. They say that beside every great trout river there is a good fly shop; I say that beside every great trout river there is a Dick Hugo poem and a bar.

I like your idea, Jim, that we should write a book about the great fishing bars, of the West: Slavey's in Ketchum. Grogan's on the Big Hole. The Quack-Quack Cafe in Melrose. It's a wonder anyone finds time for sport. "Life is short; live it up," said Nikita Khrushchev.

But don't spend too much time in the dives; the real road to paradise lies twenty miles outside Missoula in the pine-covered canyon of Rock Creek. The aspens will be turning yellow; it is the very best time of year to fish this mountain stream.

After you have exhausted your interest here, take the highway east. Drive past Deer Lodge (the state prison—nothing of interest there) and past Butte, the tough mining town that Dashiell Hammett renamed "Poisonville" in *Red Harvest*. The bordellos closed long ago but the Irish saloons survive and you can still buy a great pork-chop sandwich. Be sure and send me one of those postcards bearing the legend "Most Beautiful Sight in Montana"—a picture of Butte in the rear-view mirror of a car.

By then you will have left behind the densely timbered high country that lies west of the Divide and settled back into the sagebrush hills and lush hay-field valleys. The shining mountain ranges, rising out of bunchgrass plains, stand miles apart, and there is a sense of light and openness to everything.

Drive to Livingston, nestled under the Beartooths and Crazy Mountains. Hang around for a few days. Drink in the bar in the old hotel where Sam Peckinpah once roomed. Despite the many faux ranches owned by movie stars and television anchormen, this is still a western cattleman's and railroader's town. Go down to Mallard's Rest on the Yellowstone River, where the jagged peaks of the Absarokas rise above the dark timberline. If you have timed this right, the bankside cottonwoods and willows will be turning September yellow against a blue spangled stream. If you plan a float trip, this is the time and the river to do it on. Linger long after dark. Listen to the passing Canada geese. Watch for an early moonrise over the Absarokas, so bright you can count the cattle by it.

Go down to West Yellowstone, Montana, a little town that looks like an inverted pinball machine leaning up against the western entrance to the park. This must be the trout-fishing capital of the Western Hemisphere. The town of nine hundred year-round residents supports five fly shops.

As for Yellowstone Park, what can I say? You will want to fish the Firehole on cold overcast days. Watch for buffalo in the lower basins. Observe the bright algae living in the boiling hot pools. Breathe deep the hydrogen sulfide, the "rotten egg gas," which escapes from vents in the earth. Listen to the whine of brine flies mating and dying in the humid warmth just above a hot pool. Count the skeletons of dead birds lying beside the poison springs. You have never seen a trout river like this, have you, you old Swamp Yankee? Look at the soft swirls and rings the Firehole trout make inhaling insects in the weedy current. This water is a wilderness of its own, full of secret life, mysteries we can only imagine.

Fish the Madison River for butter yellow brown trout that have come up from Hebgen Lake to spawn. Try Baker's Hole—but remember this is "grizzer" country. Not too long ago a bear devoured a sleeping camper at this very spot. Imagine the existential thrill of seeing an adult male grizzly, a rippling mountain of fur rising up in front of you. Fish the brushy south fork Madison outside the park for more spawning browns from Hebgen Lake. Try the Gardiner below Sheep Eater Cliffs for brook trout with sides like jewel-inlaid mosaics. Fish Buffalo Ford on the Yellowstone for large and profoundly stupid cutthroats. The canyon of the Lewis River is particularly beautiful after a light September snowfall. Be sure and fish below its falls, if only for the backdrop. Take a day off and look at the geysers. They are best under a field of snow, the plumes and steaming roostertails rising up over the white basins. Here's a hint for viewing wildlife: elk come down to the rivers at dusk to drink. The tourists are in camp cooking supper, so you'll have the animals to yourself. At first the sight of huge elk watering so close to you will be unnerving. But in time they will seem like so many six-hundred-pound squirrels on your lawn.

Be alert for the wonderful slinking forms of coyotes. They are like the Indians in *Cheyenne Autumn* watching from the high mesa. They always see you first. At night their laughter travels across the meadows. It drives the dogs in the campgrounds crazy.

Here's some basic advice for the park.

On your *third* week in the park, slow down and fish just one river (I recommend the Firehole). Allow yourself time to get to know it well until, like Nick Adams, you can fish it in your sleep.

On your *second* week in the park, try to catch a trophy brown trout on the south fork, the Madison "behind the barns" (ask for directions at the fly shops) or in the channel of the Lewis River where it empties into the lake.

But your *first* week in the park, don't worry about catching trout. See all the rivers and animals you can. Fishing is the least part of any of this.

Now this is hard. With only a few days left, go down into Wyoming and fish the Snake River under the Grand Tetons. Or go back where you started, back to the Railroad Ranch on the Henry's Fork. It's just over the Targhee Pass.

Or you can do something truly epic and fish for steelhead. To do this you will have to drive across Idaho and into Oregon. If you fish only one steelhead river in your life, make it the North Umpqua River where it flows through the heart of a steep canyon of towering Douglas fir. You probably don't have a big enough rod for steelhead but I doubt you'll hook one anyway; remember, I've seen you fish. From Yellowstone you can drive to the North Umpqua in two days. This is Zane Grey country, Jim.

Well, that about does it for your grand western tour. Come see me in San Francisco. A man can take only so much sunlight and stars, pines and meadows. Steinbeck said San Francisco was a golden handcuff with the key thrown away. We'll hit the Barbary Coast bars and shoot liar's dice for drinks. You can spend a week in City Lights Books. We'll watch the fog blow in over the bay. We'll watch someone jump off the Golden Gate Bridge.

Your good friend,
Mike

Salmon Dreams

It has been said of California that people here are always starting up the future only to shut it down the next week. But in the little town of Monte Rio on the Russian River you are reminded instead of the past. Say an earlier era when people still hitchhiked and dressed in floppy vests and denim or wore beads and shoulder-length hair. Looking around the earthy river town on a warm September afternoon, at the hitchhikers on the old River Road, at the sunlight falling into the redwood trees, at the general funkiness of the scene, you could still believe that love was free and that there would be peace in the valley at last.

Driving along the Moscow Road on the south bank of the Russian River, heading toward Monte Rio, I spy mossy cabins and tiny bungalows buried deep in the redwood shade. The mildewed river homes seem to have been built during a bygone age of modesty and remain half-hidden in the eternal gloom of the trees. The ridges and hills around here are thick with second-growth redwood trees. Coming out over the bridge into the warm sunshine, the Rio movie theater appears on the north bank like an emblem out of a fifties childhood. A vintage sign arching out over the roadway welcomes me to Monte Rio Vacation Wonderland.

The day feels like summer. A sensuous languor lies on the valley.

In the vineyards upriver, grapes the color of desire hang in clusters from twisting zinfandel vines. Bunches of cabernet-sauvignon ripen in the sun. It will be a wine the color of passion. In the sky, skeins of geese move northward in irregular slipstreams. Bandtail pigeons roost in trees in the ridges and quail call out in the bottomlands. Despite the heat there is a stirring in the valley and a clear sense of urgency to things that reminds me of Roderick Haig-Brown's observation that autumn more than any other time is the season of movement.

Clearly it is the best time of year. There is steelhead fishing in Oregon and in the Klamath and Trinity rivers up north. And the finest trout fishing of all is about to begin on the eastern slope of the Sierra Nevada mountains. Better yet, there are salmon in the Russian River, practically in my backyard.

I would call the river a dowager. She passes by like the queen mother on procession, the riches of her valley on review. Some of the pools are salad green, almost stagnant. Others are like Brown's Pool, which seems to possess the clarity of cathedral light, especially when viewed from above on its steep northern embankment. Standing on a bluff, looking down into a pool called Watson's Log, I see a pod of salmon pass through the pool's limpid reflection.

I drive back upriver to the small resort town of Guerneville. The accordion player, an old hippie, has taken up his usual station in front of King's Sport & Tackle and I drop a dollar into his open instrument case. Inside I purchase a dozen green comet flies, peculiar to the river. Although it is early in the season, the shop's counter is lined with Polaroid snapshots of salmon taken from Moscow Pool and the Monte Rio Riffle.

I receive complicated directions for Neeley's Beach, where a half-dozen salmon have been taken on flies. The route requires me to wade the river to the south bank and then find my way around a tract of residential homes on a trail leading down to the beach. I get to Neeley's in time to join two other fly fishermen in the pool. Through an accident of harmonics, the sound of a television set drifts over to me from one of the river homes, perhaps that warping linoleum structure standing up on stilts in a tangle of undergrowth. So this is what the glory of the Pacific Ocean has come down to. I think of a salmon sharing a pool with a bicycle tire or a sheet of corrugated iron, its life force draining into the river as people walk their dogs beside the embankment. I imagine a salmon pool as a funhouse mirror reflecting scented vacation homes and landscaped subdivisions. I wade in. I cast to the opposite shore. Gradually a rhythm sets in and three fly lines weave back and forth over the water, backlit by the sun.

Still, I would call the pool sylvan. Afternoon passes and a gray-green shadow stretches out over the river. A salmon shatters the stillness and I stare into the disappearing rings where the fish momentarily surfaced. Another salmon rolls farther downstream. I feel a soft tug on my line and a spongy resistance. It is a submerged branch. I pick up and cast again and halfway through the drift I feel another tug, different this time. The feeling is unmistakable—the rod comes to life in my hands. A salmon is on!

I can feel the surge of energy, the ocean-roaming power. The salmon breaks the surface and submerges; the rod strains. For ten minutes line is surrendered and retaken; the rod bends and recovers in my hands. The salmon twists against the line, trying to thrust its way downstream. But soon I am holding a five-pound coho, a silver salmon, at my side. A hen fish, her metallic colors are already fading like washed-out polar light. I am looking down at the first salmon I have ever taken on a fly rod.

Salmon are emblems of the Pacific Northwest. More than anything else, they represent the abundance of life found here. In salmon we can see the world as a perfect circle—birth and death, the promise of return, the power of instinct. For me, a salmon leaping a waterfall is the most stirring spectacle in nature.

All Pacific salmon die after spawning. For this reason, salmon fishing, more than any other kind, seems both life-conscious and death-conscious at once. Even on a domesticated stream like the Russian River, a salmon still remains a creature of almost inexpressible mystery. This is the alpha and omega of angling.

There are five species of Pacific salmon and in California the two most abundant are kings and silver salmon. As their name implies, kings are the largest of the salmon. For years it was thought that salmon, after roaming the Pacific's gallery of wonders, were somehow able to find their way back to their home streams through their remarkable sense of smell. As if a king salmon could somehow be able to detect, through a thousand miles of open ocean, the faintest dilution of its natal streams. There have been other navigational theories, too, ranging from sonar to celestial. Scientists suspect that salmon actually navigate by means of the earth's magnetic field; portions of a salmon's brain are particularly rich in iron. Fingerling salmon, placed in a tank and subjected to an artificial magnetic field, line up in unison, like tiny compass needles. Using an inner magnetic map, and sensing pivotal changes in the earth's seasons, a school of salmon unerringly turns toward home when the time comes to procreate.

This knowledge, passed down the generations, includes feeding and schooling behavior, orientation to currents and the timing of the spawning run. Once near shore, a salmon's superior sense of scent comes into play and the fish is able to distinguish its birth river from all the others. Most likely, a salmon spawns in the very river pool where he was born.

Pacific salmon are cousins to Atlantic salmon, but any similarity between the sport as it is practiced on the West Coast and the venerable preciousness of Atlantic salmon fishing ends here. An Atlantic salmon fisherman is likely to regard a Pacific salmon fisherman as something he might dig out of his ear.

Atlantic salmon flies resemble antique Victorian embroidery and have anglophile names like Green Highlander and Durham Ranger. Pacific salmon flies look like something tied by a three-fingered logger. Atlantic salmon fishermen tend to be heart surgeons from Boston who annually reserve expensive beats on New Brunswick rivers. Pacific salmon fishermen drive beat-up pickup trucks and are deer hunters. It is *Masterpiece Theatre* versus *Hee Haw*.

Doubtless the silver salmon I caught on the Russian River was a hatchery fish. The run of wild silver salmon on that river is purely vestigial. The run of kings on the Russian is the product of hatchery mitigation, too. They are not even native to the river, having pedigrees shorter still than the newcomers to the Russian River valley who have taken up residence in split-level river duplexes and wine-country condominiums.

But there is one California river where a race of giant king salmon flourishes. They are river gods that can weigh up to fifty and even sixty pounds. That river is called the Smith and it pours in a crystal clear torrent out of the granite ribs of the Siskiyou Mountains near Oregon, where it gathers and folds into slow pools beneath a towering redwood forest. I aim to take one of these monster salmon on a fly rod, as I crave the mythological in life.

Dawn on the Early Hole. The pale sky clings to the treetops like a damp canvas tent. The ancient redwood forest is dark and indistinct, the light over the river gray as a translucent glacier. River stones shine wetly on the wide gravel bars and a balsamic odor of evergreen fills the canyon. At the top of the pool, the prams of the fishermen are lined gunnel to gunnel and the only sound over the water is the soft hiss of fly lines and an occasional low curse.

A salmon erupts from the surface of the pool with a sound like a deep cough. Below these prams, fifty to seventy-five salmon float suspended in a pool of black light.

It is going to be a bright, windless November day. Autumn has come to the Smith River canyon, and with it the salmon. They are spread throughout the river all the way up to the forks. I've been avoiding the pram lineups that are anchored above the honey holes and spend a lot of time wandering the sweeping gravel bars in search of solitude.

Mist covers the river. In the first gray light of day, the canyon appears almost ethereal. Soon bright sunshine will flood the gravel banks, warming the river stones. The pools will become vast catch basins of light, their underwater architecture revealed. Right now salmon hold at Pyramid Rock, below the Hiouchi Bridge, and in the great convex mirror of Society Hole.

The pools are pristine, the river pure as oxygen. The clarity of the water is almost alarming and makes me wonder if I will ever be able to take one of these numinous creatures on a fly rod.

The canyon is matchless: the redwoods primordial, the cliffs covered in moss and dripping lichens. Back from the rocky shelves, a thicket of damp ferns recedes into trees that are centuries old. The river's strong currents push against moss-covered rocks and fold into quiet eddies. A soft breeze soughing in the crowns of the redwoods breaks the stillness. Beyond this, the continuous roar of white water, faint and far away, rising and falling like the cheering of a distant crowd.

Frankly, the fishing is daunting. Much of the water is simply too deep to wade. And I am somewhat reluctant to venture into these crowded amphitheater pools. The faces of the fishermen, who are standing upright in their prams, seem to be set in fierce concentration. There is a wariness in the established lineup; veterans don't welcome strangers. You need the skills of a diplomat just to enter a pool. Another thing: these guys are *good*. Their lines slice through the air at incredible distances, turning over with complete authority. These are the best fly casters I've ever seen. I feel embarrassed to be among them, to reveal my own casting form, which a friend once told me displayed "flashes of mediocrity."

Clearly this is no arena for amateurs. Some of these fishermen arrived two hours before sunrise just to get into the lineup that forms over the meat bucket—the area of a salmon pool holding the largest mass of fish. Salmon enter a river in schools and hold in the deeper pools waiting for rain to raise the level of the river before moving on. Milling salmon generally concentrate on a section of a pool where they feel the most secure, favoring rocky shelves and ledges, deep slots and the protection of back eddies. On the Smith milling salmon can be spotted circling over the granite bottom in water that is astonishingly clear. Fly fishermen endeavor to drop their lures at the point where the salmon are making the turn. After a few days of this restless behavior, salmon settle closer to the bottom and hold in the current. This is when lockjaw sets in and salmon become terribly difficult to entice. Pram fishermen say that if you're not in the bucket you might as well be in the parking lot.

Clearly a degree of cooperation is required here. I saw a pram fisherman give a bank angler a ride after he couldn't control his boiling salmon from the rocks. A hooked salmon can tie up all the lines in a pool. Fishermen pull up anchor and row out of the lineup, rod between knees, before doing battle. Salmon are so large they require a net or a beach to land; some of the bigger ones can pull an eight-foot pram around the river. When the fight is over, an angler is allowed to retake his rightful place in the lineup. But if he leaves to take a piss, his spot is up for grabs. Such is the code of the river.

This kind of fishing calls for a sociability that is not part of my nature. On the chance the salmon are on the move (it rained the night before), I decide to forgo fishing for pooled-up, suspended fish and see if I can intercept a traveler in a fast-water run.

My choice is the White Horse Riffle, which in midwinter becomes a tremendous steelhead run often lined with fly fishermen. As I walk out across the wide gravel bar beneath a vast, misty tract of redwoods, my only company is the shadow a circling golden eagle throws on the stones.

I fish the heart out of the riffle, working the fly downstream like a mine sweeper, but there is nothing to write home about. Perhaps there's something to be said for orthodoxy after all.

I make the long trip across the river, to the little hamlet of Hiouchi, and find my way down to the Cable Hole, a great staging area for salmon. I have to cross a shallow channel that lies against the northern bank in order to get out to the gravel bar. On the far shore, a large granite outcropping, covered in moss and colored lichen, juts out into the river and salmon are holding below the boil. There is a premium here on distance casting.

Several fly fishermen stand in water up to their armpits firing casts at the far bank, vapor flying off their lines. One of the men is playing a salmon, one of the few hookups I have seen all day. The salmon is a fresh midnight blue and chrome; its flesh has not yet begun to turn from its stay in the river. When the heavy fall rains finally come, salmon move quickly through the forks of the Smith, carrying the torch of life into the headwaters and tributaries. But how quickly they fade. By December their blackened corpses, looking like burned-out fuselages, lie rotting along willow banks and leaf-strewn gravel bars, a feast for eagles and boar coons. But the genetic history of the run lies buried in clean river gravel in the shape of eggs ticking with life.

The sun has climbed above the wall of redwoods and the morning light slants into the river, illuminating the terraqueous outlines of submerged boulders and bedrock shelves. I fish for an hour, changing fly patterns three times. My movements are dully reflexive: pick up and cast, the line swinging convexly through the current. Except for the one salmon at the Cable Hole, and the tuneful glide of water against the banks, things are a little slow.

I eat my lunch on the gravel bar downriver at Simpson Park, where someone beached a forty-pounder earlier this morning. I can only imagine the flash of color and roiling energy of such a fish. How overwhelming it must have felt to pull a king salmon that size out of the river.

It is said that more salmon over fifty pounds are taken out of the Smith River on a fly rod than in all other Northwest rivers combined. No doubt an exaggeration, but the point is well taken. It was long believed king salmon, because they hold so deeply, couldn't even be caught on a fly rod. That was before pioneer fly fishermen—guys like Jim Adams, Bob Weddell and the great Bill Schaadt —began experimenting with leadcore shooting heads in the Smith River and proved the conventional wisdom wrong. Those lines were crudely patched together out of trolling line and lead wire and the effect was like trying to swing a cable. Today there are any number of commercially available lines that not only cast effortlessly but will get you down to the salmon. So this kind of fishing has become accessible to more people. Which is either good or bad, depending on how you view these things.

An osprey soars overhead and vine maples along the bank bleed their colors into the river. Afternoon dissolves in the music of rapids and the leisurely swing of lines across the pools. Towering redwood monarchs reflect up through black-green depths. Now and again, a giant salmon causes a guttural eruption, shattering the still mirror of a pool.

There comes a moment in the day when the late-afternoon light strikes the river at such an abrupt angle that everything suddenly becomes luminous but indistinct. And then the sun drops below a wall of redwoods, and underwater boulders and cave-like grottos once visible disappear under an expressive lid of shadow.

Finally a fly fisherman, standing directly above me, brings his rod up on a salmon. There is a furious boil of water just below the surface. Naturally I have mixed feelings about this. I can't help but think that, given a little more time, *that* could have been my fish.

There is a sharp protest from the angler's reel as the salmon tears across the pool, throwing a grand wake. For a quarter of an hour there is head-shaking and churning on the bottom of the pool. Finally the angler manages to beach his salmon on the gravel bar.

"How big is it?" I ask.

"About eighteen pounds."

Average size for the river. The dorsal is a greenish black and its sides are like bright chain mail. The fisherman slips the salmon back into the river.

It is a hollow feeling not to be catching salmon. The poet Rilke said that if the wine is bitter, become the wine. I decide that if I have to resent someone taking a fish while I go blank then I have no business even being near rivers. And if I can't appreciate salmon running upstream in a suburban freshet like the Russian, my home river, when it is the color of mini-mart coffee, then I probably don't deserve miracles either. I want to live the fullest possible life I can today. Now.

A cold dusk settles around me. The sky above the canyon is a deep twilight blue. Cries of exultation rise from the prams. The salmon are on! I fish without a strike until the canyon grows pitch dark and the stars come out above the black evergreens.

I inhale the stars. They fill me up.

About the Author

Michael Checchio is a former newspaperman turned freelance writer and dedicated fly fisherman. His journalism has appeared in such publications as *The New York Times* and *The National Law Journal*. His sporting essays have been published in magazines such as *Gray's Sporting Journal* and *Fly Rod & Reel*. Born in Maine, he grew up near the pinelands and barrier islands of southern New Jersey. He resides in San Francisco and lives for the fly-fishing rivers of the West.